Nathaniel Bacon

*Artist
Gentleman
and Gardener*

Karen Hearn

Tate Publishing

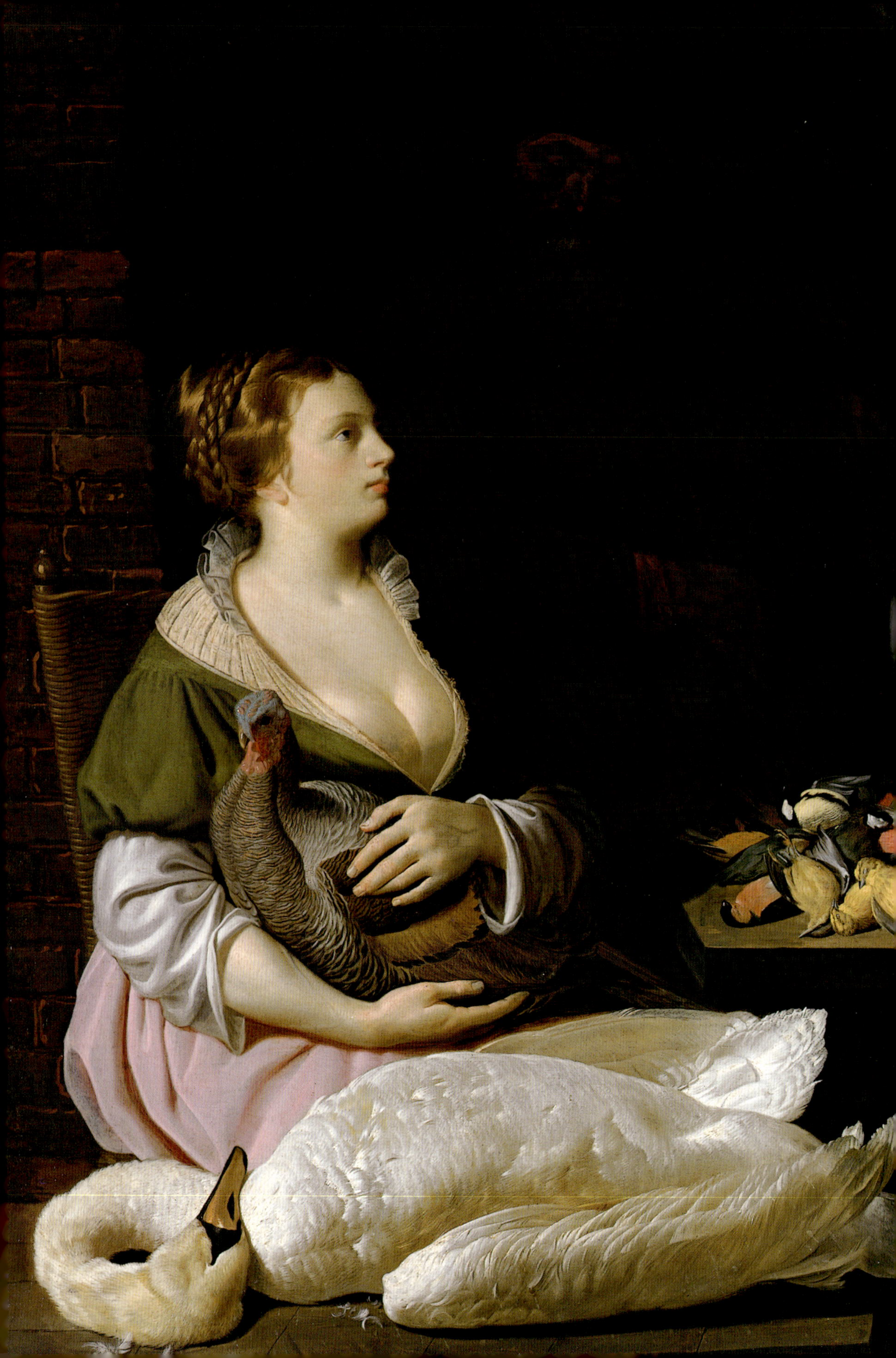

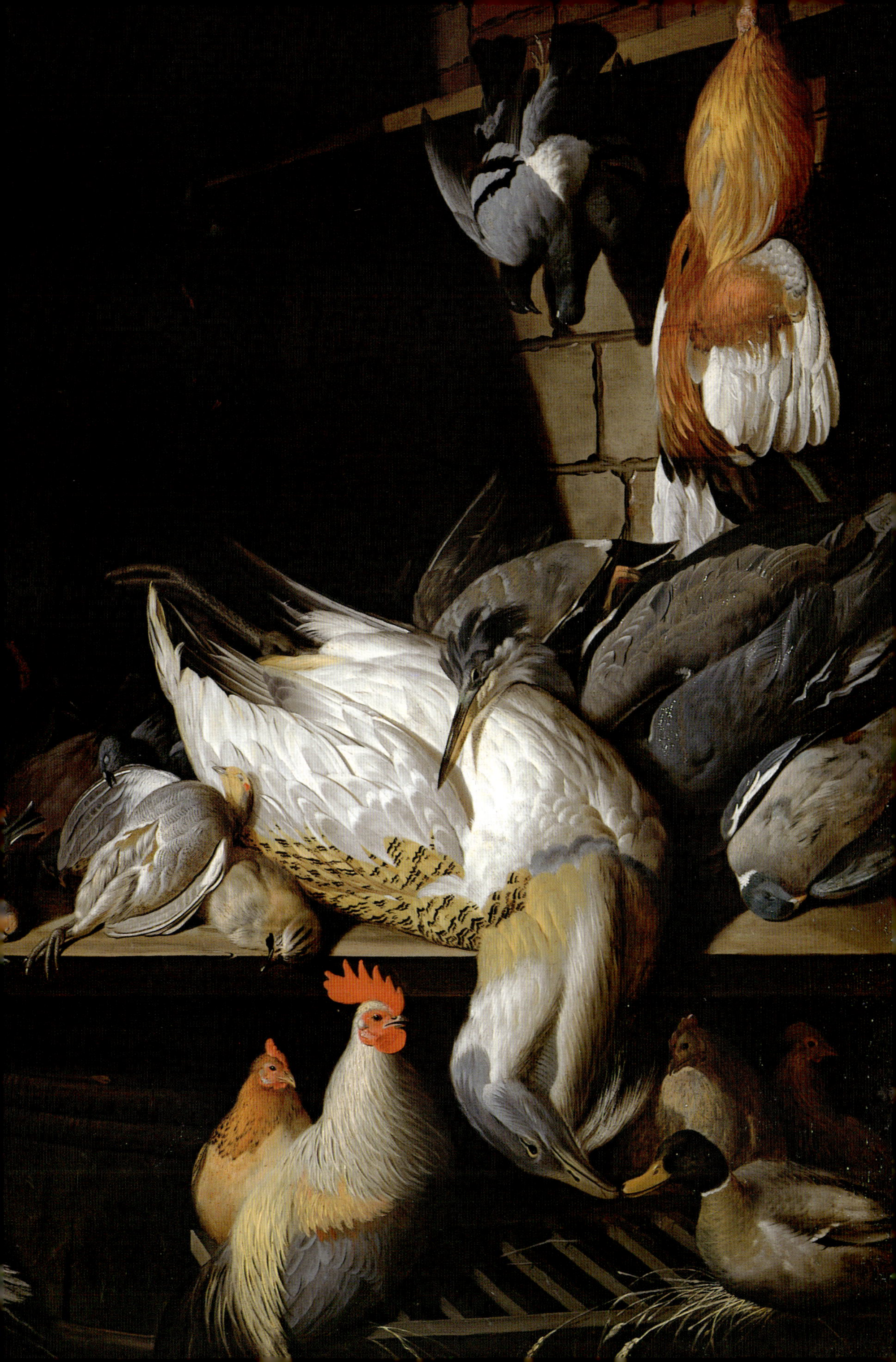

Published to accompany
the exhibition at Tate Britain,
14 November 2005 –
17 April 2006

First published 2005 by
order of the Tate Trustees
by Tate Publishing, a division
of Tate Enterprises Ltd,
Millbank, London
SW1P 4RG
www.tate.org.uk/publishing

British Library Cataloguing
in Publication Data
A catalogue record for
this book is available
from the British Library

ISBN 1-85437-637-3

Designed by
Matt Brown at Branch
Printed by
South Seas
International Press

Front cover:
*Cookmaid with Still Life
of Vegetables and Fruit*
(detail of fig.11)

Back cover:
Self-Portrait
(detail of fig.9)

Frontispiece (fig.1):
*Cookmaid with
Still Life of Birds*
Oil on canvas 188 × 236 cm
Private Collection

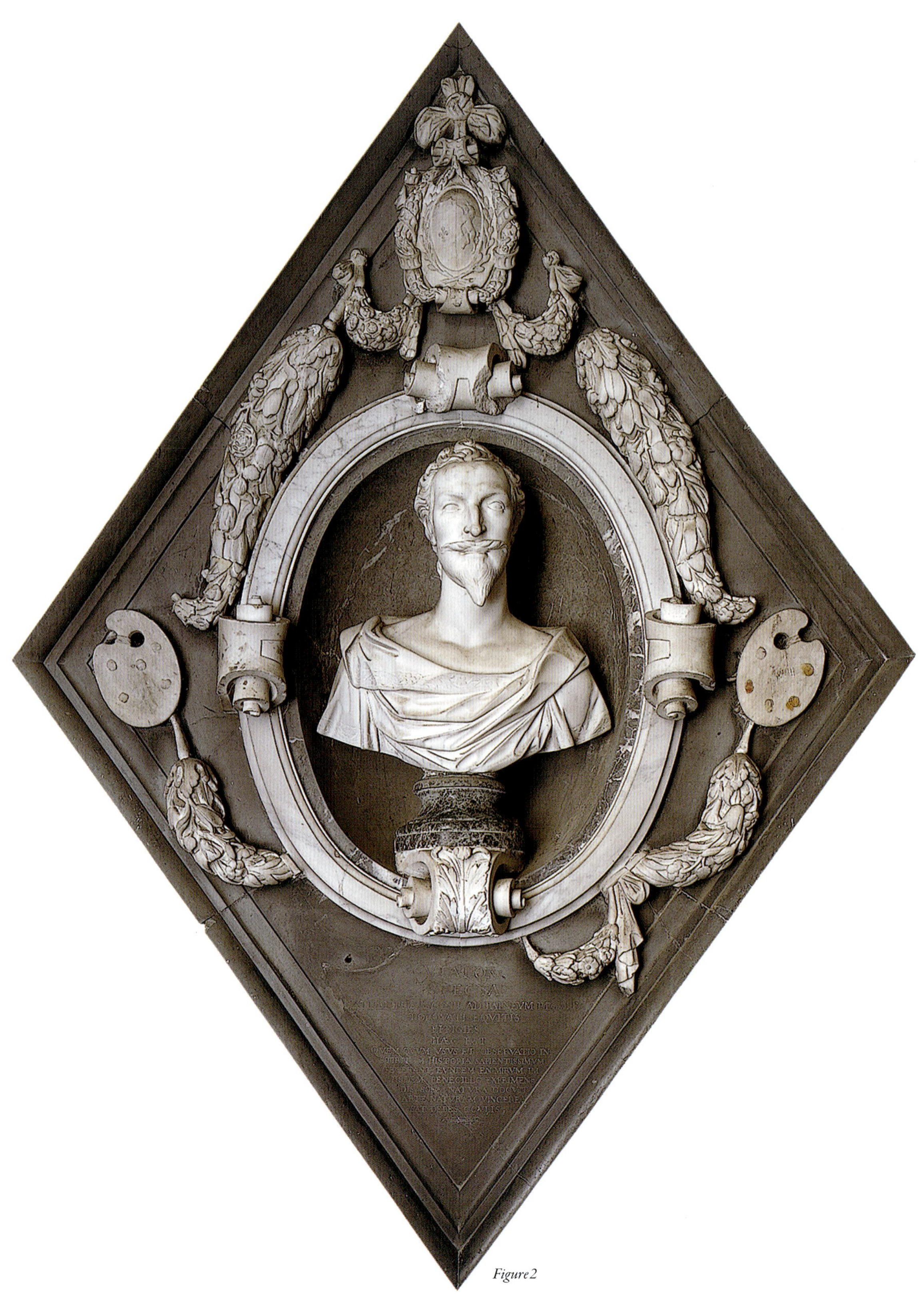

Figure 2

On 1 July 1627 – only two years into the reign of King Charles I – Sir Nathaniel Bacon, gentleman, died at the age of forty-one.[1] A few months later, it was reported that his funerary monument was 'well under way' in London (fig.2). It was being made by the most fashionable sculptor to the Court, the Netherlandish-trained Englishman, Nicholas Stone.[2] It was subsequently installed in St Mary's Church at Culford – adjoining one of Bacon's residences, Culford Hall in Suffolk. Although moved to a new position in the mid-nineteenth century, the monument remains in Culford Church to this day. Exceptionally, for a monument of this period – and particularly for one to a gentleman – it includes two carved representations of a painter's palettes.[3] It is an elegant construction – and in artistic terms it was cutting edge. The deceased is shown as if in classical attire, in emulation of a piece of Roman sculpture. The monument bears a Latin inscription, which can be translated as follows: 'Look Traveller, this is the monument of Nathaniel Bacon, A Knight of the Bath, whom, when experience and observation had made him most knowledgeable in the history of plants, astonishingly, Nature alone taught him through his experiments with the brush to conquer Nature by Art. You have seen enough. Farewell.'[4]

This short book will outline the known details and extent of Bacon's career and works. With the exception of a tiny painting on metal, his oeuvre has been established largely through family tradition, underpinned by stylistic comparison, with only nine surviving paintings commonly agreed to be by Bacon. The nature of the claims made on Bacon's monument will also be examined in an attempt to reveal why and in what context they were made.

Born at Redgrave, near Diss, in Suffolk in late August 1585, Bacon was a nephew of the politician, natural philosopher and writer, Sir Francis Bacon. The Bacon dynasty had been elevated only comparatively recently by Nathaniel's grandfather, Sir Nicholas Bacon. The son of the head shepherd for the Abbey of Bury St Edmunds, Sir Nicholas had studied at Cambridge, where he established a lifelong friendship with William Cecil, later Lord Burghley. After a legal training at Gray's Inn, he progressed via various law appointments through to Queen Elizabeth I's Privy Council, becoming Lord Keeper of the Great Seal (and, effectively, Lord Chancellor). His second marriage made him brother-in-law to Burghley, who was by then principal adviser to the Queen. Sir Nicholas died in 1579, six years before Nathaniel was born. Nathaniel's father was a son of the Lord Keeper by his first wife; also named Nicholas, he was subsequently to become the 'premier' baronet of England under James I. This title marks the fact that he was the first ever baronet to be created.

Nathaniel the painter was the youngest of nine sons and two daughters – well born into a newly elevated family, but with uncertain future prospects. He was raised at Redgrave Hall in Suffolk. At his marriage on 1 May 1614 he acquired from his parents nearby Culford Hall (built *c.*1586–91, but rebuilt in the eighteenth century) and its estates, four miles north of Bury St Edmunds. He also gained Brome Hall (wholly demolished in the twentieth century) in the same county through his wife, who had inherited it from her first husband. Culford and Brome were about twenty miles apart. Nathaniel had fulfilled a younger son's family duty to make a good marriage, for Jane Meautys, Lady Cornwallis, was a rich widow. Before her first marriage she had been an attendant on Anne of Denmark, James I's queen. Jane's first husband, Sir William Cornwallis, of Brome and of Highgate – then just outside London – had died in 1611, leaving her with an infant son, Frederick. The fact that Queen Anne was godmother to this boy indicates Jane's status. The wealth and property that she brought appear to have given Bacon the freedom not to attend at Court, to remain in Suffolk doing what he pleased, and to travel. The couple were to have three children: Anne (1615–80), Nicholas (1617–60) and Jane, born 1624, who died less than four months after her father.[5] Only Anne was to have any offspring although none of these lived to adulthood.

The main source of the personal information about Bacon that survives is a group of letters relating to his wife Jane.[6] Some are written by Bacon himself and seem to be the earliest surviving *personal* letters (as opposed to business correspondence) by an English artist. They indicate that he was a devoted family man, fascinated with political developments in northern Europe, and rather interested in his own health (fig.3). Jane's other correspondents included Lucy Harington, Countess of Bedford, a Lady of the Bedchamber to Anne of Denmark, one of the most powerful women at Court, and an art collector on her own account.[7]

The letters show that Bacon himself travelled to the Low Countries. For example, his mother wrote in 1613 that he was about to go 'beyond the seas … so as we are content to lett hym travell for his recreation' – so he was specifically not going on business.[8] On 29 November that year he was at Gravesend 'ready to depart for Flushing' and giving directions as to how he could be contacted in Antwerp. Later, in 1620, the Countess of Bedford wrote enquiring whether she might meet up with him at The Hague that summer, in terms that suggest that he may have been a regular visitor there.[9]

The surviving correspondence contains no direct references by Bacon to his painting activities. The nearest possibility comes on 6 February 1614, when he writes from Suffolk to his fiancée Jane, who was in London: 'Speak yo(e) mynde to the Lady of Bedford in my behalf, and tell her that the weather hath bin very unfavorable to the proceedinges of her picture.' It is not absolutely clear what this means – whether Bacon was painting a work for her, or supervising the production of one by someone else, or even importing one from overseas.

He does make a couple of references, in May 1624, to the ordering of 'coullers' – i.e. pigments. They are to be sent from London by one John Fenn who seems to have been in the employ of the Bacons (he was to witness the artist's will in 1627). In the first case, Bacon asks for '3 oz more masticott [a form of yellow]', but 'it need not be of the best sort', as it was needed for decorative purposes, for painting a chair or seat.[10]

The most informative early documentary reference to specific pictures by Bacon is in the inventory connected with his wife's will, of 1659, 'Ten, Great peeces [i.e. big pictures] in Wainscoate of fish and fowle &c done by Sr: Nath: Bacon', which hung 'On the great Stayere [Stair] and in the Gallery' at Culford.[11] (For a transcript of the part of this inventory that lists the paintings at Culford, see p.32.) *Cookmaid with Still Life of Birds*, still in the possession of the artist's indirect descendants at Gorhambury, Herts, is traditionally thought to be one of these (fig.1, frontispiece). It was first noted at Gorhambury by the engraver and antiquary George Vertue in 1720–1. A less sophisticated visitor who saw it in 1731, John Loveday of Caversham, commented on 'A very good Piece in another Room drawn by Sir Nathaniel Bacon who was no Limner [i.e. painter] but took a fancy to the Cook-maid of the House; whom he draws sitting, a Fellow behind her who has brought in Fowl, the several kinds of which are exactly represented.'[12] Another is the *Cookmaid*

Sweet Hart

I reciued yo[e] leter wherby I understand of the slowp[ro]ceeding
of y[e] business & for myne owne part her I cannot be so
well pleased but I must desier dayly to be w[th] you wherfore
I desier you to send I me word by the next whether my
comminge may be inconuenient or not & how longe you
meane to stay. for my cominge I cannot wright any
thinge certayne for my horses ar infected wth other
sick horses & so extreame sick that I know not
whether they will liue or not. for my health I cannot
wright as I did last for this last week I suffered more
payne in my teeth then euer & this night I slept
not one hower & am now goinge to the Mountebanck
at Bury to draw them out for y[e] children they ar
in very good health. Nick sends you word of a brood
of young chickens & of a disaster he escaped at my
beinge wth him for he eate so much milk porrage ^at supper^ ther
he cryed out (o lord) I think I haue almost broake
myne gault: & I was fayne to walk him a turne
or iy about the chamber to digest yt

newes I cann wright none wherfore I desier you onely
to entertayne my earnest desiere to enioy yo[ur] compeny
then w[ch] nothing can be more pleasing to him who
is & shalbe alwaies onely

                              yo[u]r[s] nath[.] Bacon

with Still Life of Game, re-acquired by Bacon's descendants in the 1950s (fig.13, p.23).[13] The Tate *Cookmaid with Still Life of Vegetables and Fruit c.*1620–5 may be a third from this set (fig.11, p.23).[14] No other British artist of the early seventeenth century painted still lifes.[15]

On an entirely different scale from the immense *Cookmaids* is a tiny work also thought to be by Bacon, measuring only 7.1 × 10.7 cm (fig.4). Painted in oil on copper, *Landscape* bears the conjoined monogram 'NB' (in the tree). It was presumably painted during the 1620s and has been in the collection of the Ashmolean Museum, Oxford, since its foundation in the late seventeenth century. It is thought to be the 'small Landskip drawn by Sir Nath: Bacon' that in 1656 was listed in an inventory of the collection amassed largely by the celebrated gardener John Tradescant the Elder.[16] If so, it is the first-known pure landscape painting by an English-born artist. Bacon was closely related to Robert Cecil, 1st Earl of Salisbury (the son of William Cecil, Lord Burghley), who had been the patron of Tradescant.

Freely painted in a range of impasto greens, browns and greys, this little picture shows a tree-topped rock at the centre, up which ascend a tiny horseman and a figure on foot. Buildings are seen to the right, cottages to the left and a church behind, with another on the horizon. The composition is possibly intended to represent the Flight into Egypt of Mary and Joseph, but the figures are too minute to be certain. It should be noted that no signature or monogram has so far been found on any other work by Bacon. The ebony frame appears to be original to this work.

Landscape painting had previously been practised in Britain only by Netherlandish artists. Indeed, the painter and herald, Edward Norgate, in his early seventeenth-

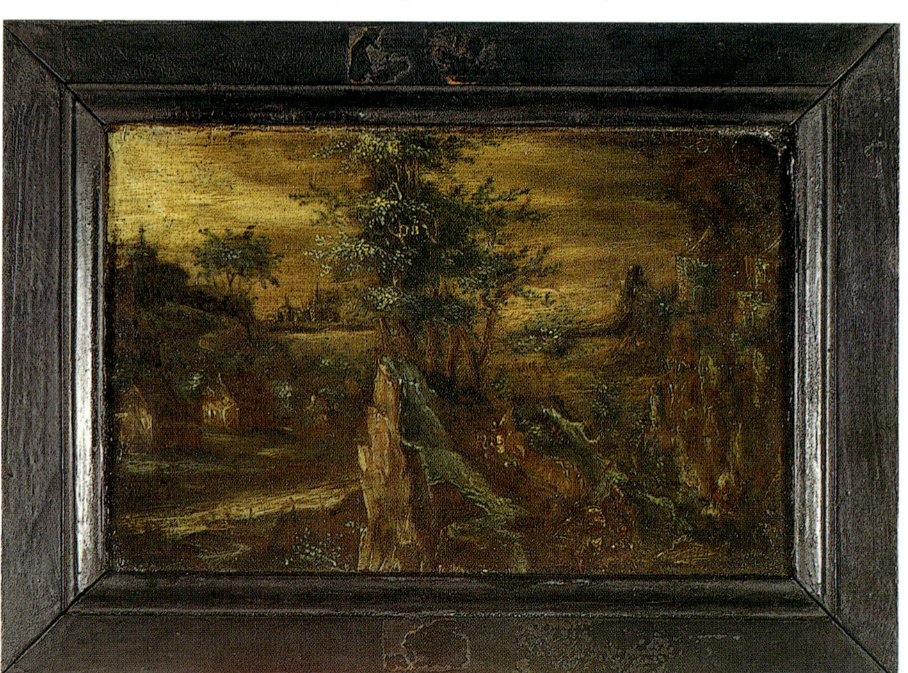

Figure 4

4
Landscape 1620s
bearing the conjoined
monogram 'NB'
Oil on copper 7.1 × 10.7 cm
The Ashmolean
Museum, Oxford

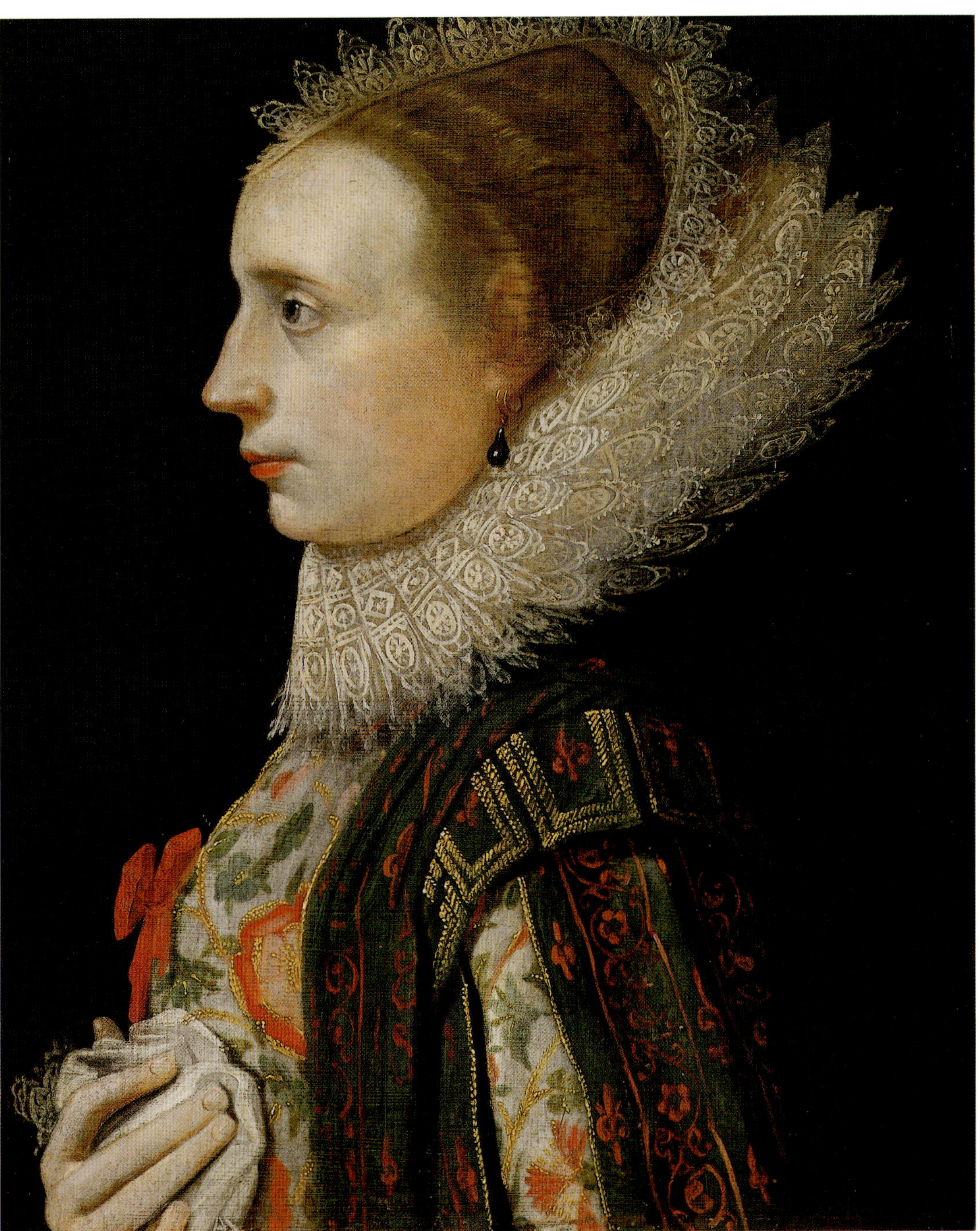

Figure 5

5
Portrait of a Lady, possibly
Jane Bacon
Oil on panel 60×49.5 cm
Private Collection

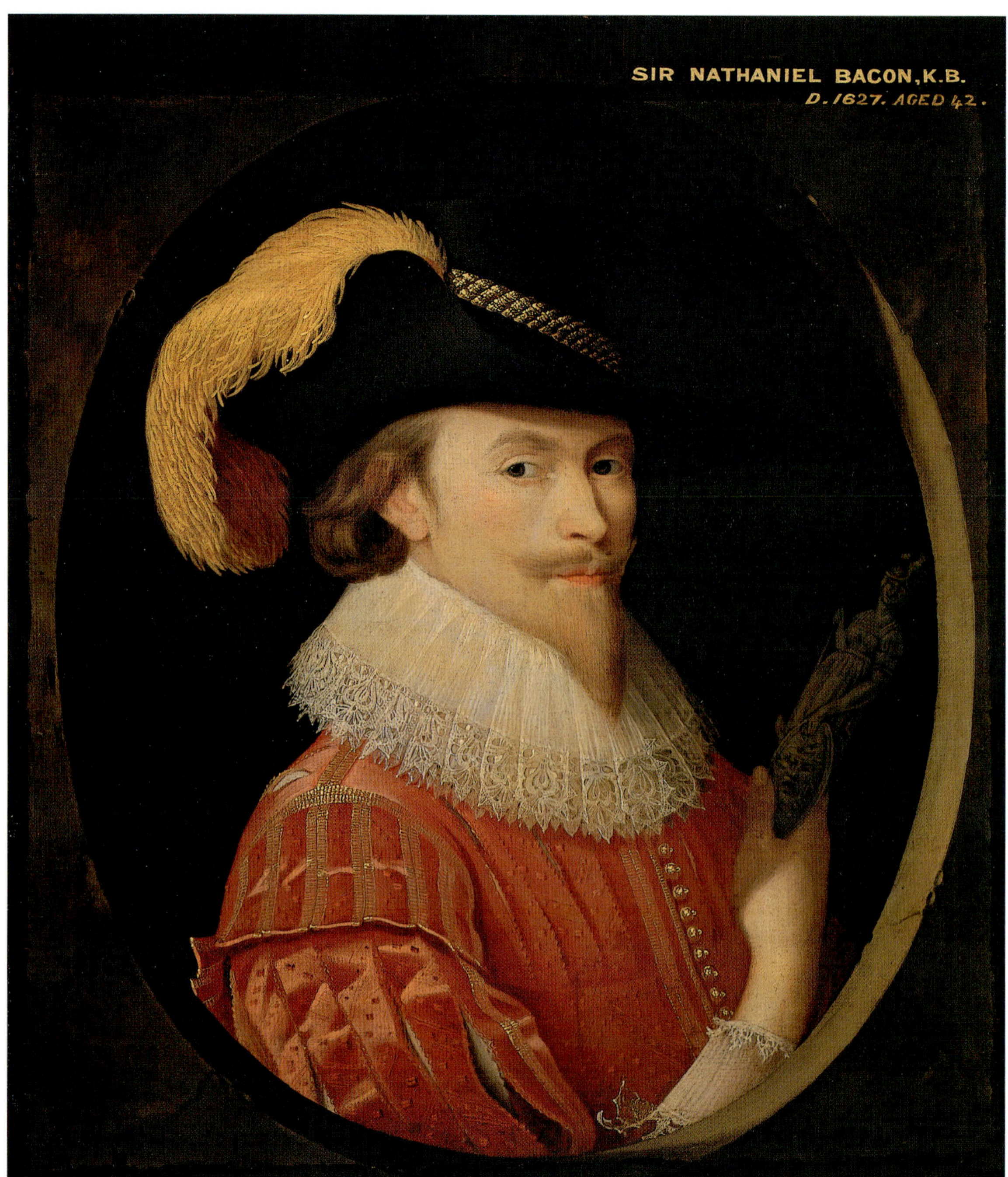

Figure 6

6
Self-Portrait
Oil on canvas 75×62.3 cm
Private Collection

century manuscript treatise 'Miniatura', described it as 'an Art soe new in England, and soe lately come a shore, as all the Language within our fower Seas cannot find it a Name, but a borrowed one from the Dutch' – i.e. 'landschap'. Norgate also commended the work of Adam Elsheimer and Paul Brill, examples of whose small paintings on copper were owned by the most active English art collectors of the early seventeenth century, including Thomas Howard, Earl of Arundel and Charles I.

A head-and-shoulders profile portrait of a lady attired in the fashion of about 1620 is by family tradition said to depict Bacon's wife, although it had previously, implausibly, been said to be of his mother, who had died in 1616 (fig.5). In addition, in 1780 William Musgrave's informant Thomas Kerrich recorded at Culford a painting of 'Lady Bacon, with Boy, & 2 Children [altered to 'daughters'] all whole figures, in the background a view of Broom Hall, from ye Garden This Picture was over the Chimney in the Gallery at Brome. This Lady brought the Culford Estates into the Cornwallis family.' It is tempting to speculate that this family portrait – whose whereabouts are now unknown – might have been by her husband.[17]

Apart from the above works, the remaining securely attributed surviving paintings by Sir Nathaniel Bacon are self-portraits. Probably the earliest, which has descended in another branch of the family, is a head-and-shoulders in a feigned oval, dating, to judge from the falling lace ruff, to about 1619 (fig.6). The inscription, top right, was added much later. Bacon gazes out directly, engaging the viewer's full attention. He is expensively and fashionably attired in mulberry-coloured satin – and there is a distinct sense of showing-off in the upward flick of the satin shoulder piece and of the lace edging the wrist-cuff. It is an expression of the 'nonchalance' required of a gentleman. He grasps a small piece of sculpture, classical in design, which appears to be of the Greek goddess Pallas Athene (Minerva in Roman mythology) who represents learning, wisdom and the arts (see fig.10).[18]

A slightly later head-and-shoulders self-portrait, belonging to the National Portrait Gallery, London (on view at Montacute House), for whom it was recently conserved by Jenny Archbold, is a more conventional work for this period (fig.7). Bacon is equally richly attired in satin, but this time without the hat with an ebullient feather. This exposes his receding hairline. A comparable hairline is seen in the marble bust on his monument, and it is possible that a portrait similar to this one could have been used by Nicholas Stone as the basis for making the head of that figure.

Another version of the NPG portrait, in a private collection, must postdate February 1626 for it shows Bacon in a green satin jacket, wearing the red ribbon of the Order of the Bath, to which he was appointed on the occasion of Charles I's coronation that month. One may speculate that the harsher handling of this latter work could reflect the debilitating effects upon Bacon's skill of the 'long languishing desease', of which he was reported to have died.[19]

Before considering Bacon's largest and most complex self-portrait in detail, it is important to remember how few self-portraits by artists working in Britain survive from the sixteenth century. Gerlach Flicke was a German painter who worked in Britain from about 1545, soon after the death of Hans Holbein II here, until his own death in 1558. In early 1555 Flicke is thought to have painted a tiny double portrait, showing himself with a gentleman-pirate called Henry Strangwish, about 8.9 × 12.1 cm in size.[20] In other words, it is almost a miniature. In 1577 the English-born middle-

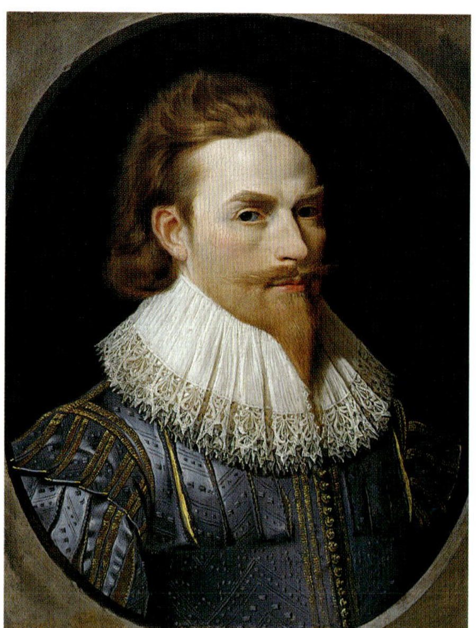

Figure 7

class portrait miniaturist and medallist, Nicholas Hilliard, made an elegant self-portrait miniature (now in the V&A). Then aged about thirty, he shows himself finely dressed – as a gentleman, rather than as an artist; in his treatise about miniature-painting in water-bound pigments, Hilliard was keen to emphasise that it was an activity for which gentlemen were best suited.[21] About thirteen years later, the French-born limner Isaac Oliver portrayed himself in equally dashing style.[22] Both these works are miniatures.

In terms of large-scale painting, one might compare and contrast Nathaniel Bacon with the earlier George Gower, Serjeant-Painter to Elizabeth I. Gower was the grandson of Sir John Gower of Stettenham in Yorkshire and thus of upper gentry stock. It is not known where or with whom Gower trained but by the 1570s he was a leading portraitist in London. In his self-portrait of 1579,[23] he presented the two principal elements of his public persona – the gentleman and the

practising artist – in a manner that challenged his contemporaries' view that these would normally be considered incompatible. He depicted himself holding a paint-charged brush and a palette on which a range of pigments were laid out, while above, in the pans of a carefully observed metal balance, a pair of dividers is shown outweighing the Gower family coat of arms. Gower stated his personal manifesto in the verse at the top:

> Thogh yovthfull wayes me did intyse,
>   From armes and uertew e[ke]
> yet thanckt be God for his god gift, wch
>   long did rest as slepe
> Now skill reuyues wth gayne, and lyfe
>   to leade in rest
> by pensils trade, wherfore I must,
>   esteme of it as best
> The proof wherof thies ballance show,
>   and armes my birth displayes
> what Parents bare by iust re[n]owme,
>   my skill mayntenes the prayes
> And them whose vertew, fame and acts,
>   haue won for me this shield
> I reuerence muche wth seruyce eke,
>   and thanks to them do yield.

In other words, Gower felt that he needed to protest that his gentleman status, achieved by his forebears and proved by the Gower family arms, was not compromised by his practice of a craft.

However, in the years following the making of Gower's self-portrait, the ideas previously advanced in Baldassare Castiglione's *Il Cortegiano* (The Courtier), published in Italy in 1527 (and in English translation in 1561), had begun to take root in England. These privileged drawing and painting as polite arts appropriate to a gentleman. By the early years of the seventeenth century, both drawing and collecting works of art were becoming markers for the new fashion in aristocratic

7
Self-Portrait *c*.1625
Oil on panel 57.5 × 44.5 cm
National Portrait Gallery,
London

behaviour. These developments were articulated by Henry Peacham in successive publications. It was Peacham who introduced the term 'virtuoso' to the English language – a gentleman whose scholarly appreciation of the arts was one indication of his elite status. Such a gentleman would bring to all his activities what Castiglione termed *sprezzatura* – an easy nonchalance that gave the impression that no effort was needed.

In *The Compleat Gentleman* (1622) (fig.8) Henry Peacham specifically named Bacon – and Bacon alone – as the prime example of an English gentleman who could draw and paint.[24] In the chapter 'Of Drawing, Limning and Painting' Peacham first established the classical precedents of the gentleman, beginning with Aristotle, progressing through Pliny and expanding the argument with an account of the Roman nobleman Quintus Fabius, who had also been cited by Hilliard and who (according to Peacham)

although he was most honourably descended, honoured with many Titles … excellently learned in the lawes …; yet he thought his skill in painting added to these Honours, and his memory would heare the better of posteritie, for that he was endued with so excellent a qualitie …

Nor can I overpasse the ingenuity and excellency of many Nobles and Gentlemen of our owne nation herein, of whom I know many: but none in my opinion, who deserveth more respect and admiration for his skill and practice herein than Master Nathaniel Bacon of Broome in Suffolke … not inferiour in my judgement to our skilfullest Masters … that right noble and ancient family … produceth like delicate fruits from one stem so many excellent in severall qualities, that no one … family in England can say the like.

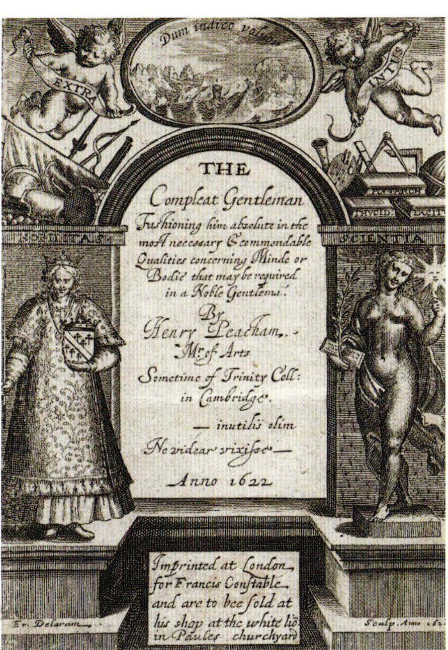

Figure 8

Peacham is here breathing life into the commonplace imagery of the family tree. Peacham's nomination of him in a book that had widespread currency must have brought Nathaniel Bacon's activities to the notice of many of his peers.

Nicholas Hilliard had advanced the view that 'limning' – painting in miniature using pigment in a water-based medium – was of greater esteem than oil painting. In the penultimate decade of the sixteenth century John Stow had written that painting was 'a meere mestier [trade] of an Artificer and handy Craftsman'. Peacham's view on this is a little more ambivalent, for he states that

Painting in Oyle is done I confess with greater iudgement [sic], and is generally of more esteeme than working in watercolours; but then … it is more Mechanique and will robbe you of over much time from your more excellent studies, it being sometime a fortnight or a month ere you can finish an ordinary peece … so curious is the workemanship to doe it well: beside, oyle nor oyle-colours, if they drop upon apparell, wil not out; when watercolours will with the least washing. But lest you should thinke mee ignorant or envious, I will not conceale from you the manner of working herein, and though it may be you shall not practise it, it may profit others.

So Peacham's line is that while the *product* of the oil painting process is of greater esteem, the actual process is not.

What Peacham was in fact doing was advising his notional gentleman reader to train himself, through practice, following guidelines from his text.[25] There was no suggestion of undergoing any form of training with a professional practitioner. Peacham's methods are, he says, 'mine owne, not borrowed out of the shops [i.e. professional workshops], but the very same Nature acquainted me withall from a child'. The inscription on Bacon's monument adopts the same line: his gentlemanly quality enabled him to devise artistic procedures himself, without advice from an artisan professional. His gentlemanly status required that this should be the spin presented.

No documentary evidence survives as to whether Bacon did receive any practical training. From the evidence of his surviving works – Netherlandish in style and subject matter – it seems likely that he must have had some form of tuition in the Low Countries. Ironically, however, what might be called the 'amateurish' aspects of his technique help to identify works as by his hand. He seems at least partly to have made the compositions up as he went along. Thus, he did not necessarily leave reserves – unpainted areas – as would a professional painter, who would need to save time and unnecessary labour, but often fully painted in a particular element (such as a wall composed of stone blocks) and then painted another item on top of it.

Bacon's experiments with the brush, as referred to on his monument, were not confined to his subject matter.[26] He also apparently experimented with pigments and varnishes, developing and perfecting new examples. From the reception of these items it is clear that he must have been in touch with professional painters who were working for the Court. Edward Norgate credited Bacon with inventing a particular 'pinke', which, confusingly, is a seventeenth-century term for 'yellow'. The principal constituent was a species of *Genista* now called 'Dyer's Greenwood'. Norgate transcribed the recipe for it in full, and noted: 'it was a Colour soe usefull and soe hard to get good as gave occasion to my late Deare Friend Sir Nathaniell Bacon … to make or finde a way to make Pincke soe very good'.[27] Norgate added that his own kinsman, Peter Oliver, son of the portrait-miniaturist Isaac Oliver, and a distinguished limner in his own right, thought so well of it that 'he used none other to his dyeing day'. One of Peter Oliver's main tasks for Charles I was to make small watercolour copies of the king's collection of Italian Old Master paintings. Norgate reported that Oliver mixed Bacon's yellow with Indian lake, to obtain 'deepe and glowing shadows'. The other principal professional portrait-miniaturist of the 1620s and 1630s, John Hoskins, also used Bacon's yellow.[28] Examination of paint sampled from the Tate *Cookmaid with Still Life of Vegetables and Fruit* (fig.11) has shown that, in mixtures to produce greens, Bacon used yellow pigment deriving from Dyer's Greenwood – in other words, his own 'pinke'.[29] A manuscript in the British Library includes Sir Nathaniel Bacon's recipe for Venice turpentine varnish for oil paintings; and this recipe must have had some currency, because it is recorded that it was subsequently used by Antony Van Dyck.[30]

It also appears that Bacon was prepared to advise his friends and peers on aesthetic issues, and probably even to supply them with works of art. In 1618 Lady Bedford was looking to him for advice on pictures: his 'judgement is so extraordinary good as I know nonne can better tell what is worth the having'. In a subsequent letter she thanked him for helping her with 'some good pieses of paintinge'.[31] Following his death, letters from his wife's cousin allude to a painting over which Bacon seems to have been acting as intermediary for Edward Sackville, 4th Earl of Dorset.[32]

In the 1630s, Philip Woodhouse, a poetically inclined suitor to the artist's daughter Anne, described the painting-filled ambience of her parents' home:

> Some pieces were by forrayne
>   Masters wrought,
> Some by ye moderne pencils of our land
> Others from Italy were safely brought
> The best was drawne by his
>   deer-loving hand
> Who more than by Apelles arte
>   had limn'd.[33]

The final two lines presumably refer to Anne's late father.

Bacon's great full-length self-portrait of about 1620 (fig.9) can be seen as a visual articulation of Peacham's 'Compleat Gentleman'.[34] Bacon sits, or rather reclines nonchalantly, revealing the elegant turn of a leg, clad in stockings of the colour he had made his own – yellow. His expensive satin attire and lace defy Peacham's warning that oil paint on apparel will not wash out. An obediently seated dog gazes up at him in an adoring attitude, which by now had become a symbol of a nobleman's authority.

Bacon asserts his rank in his self-presentation as a virtuoso. He holds what now appears to be a blank sheet of paper, but may originally have shown a drawing (or possibly an engraving). Further papers suggesting optical or perspective experiments lie on the table among the books, which signal diverse sources of learning. The pens in the inkwell imply his authorship of these drawings. Propped up is a vellum-bound book of maps, open at an edition of Abraham Ortelius's *Theatrum Orbis Terrarum …*, published some years previously in Antwerp, showing a double-page spread of Germany, which at this date included Bohemia.[35] The choice of this map suggests that Bacon was expressing his support for James I's daughter Elizabeth (with whom Lady Bedford and so many others in Bacon's circle were closely associated) and her husband Frederick, the Elector Palatine, who in 1619 was elected the king of Bohemia. In August 1620 Habsburg troops invaded the Palatinate, driving Elizabeth and Frederick into exile at The Hague. Moreover, Nathaniel's brother-in-law Sir Thomas Meautys (died 1649) was a soldier who spent most of his career fighting in the Low Countries for the Protestant cause in which the Elector Palatine played a pivotal role.

On the shelf above are further objects that define Bacon's personal status as a virtuoso: a group of small terracotta classical sculptures, the sword that denotes his gentlemanly status and, next to it, brushes and a painter's palette charged with pigments and ready for action. This assembly of items might be compared with Peacham's title page (fig.8), which shows at top left weaponry symbolic of the military role expected of a gentleman (*Nobilita*) and at top right the tools of

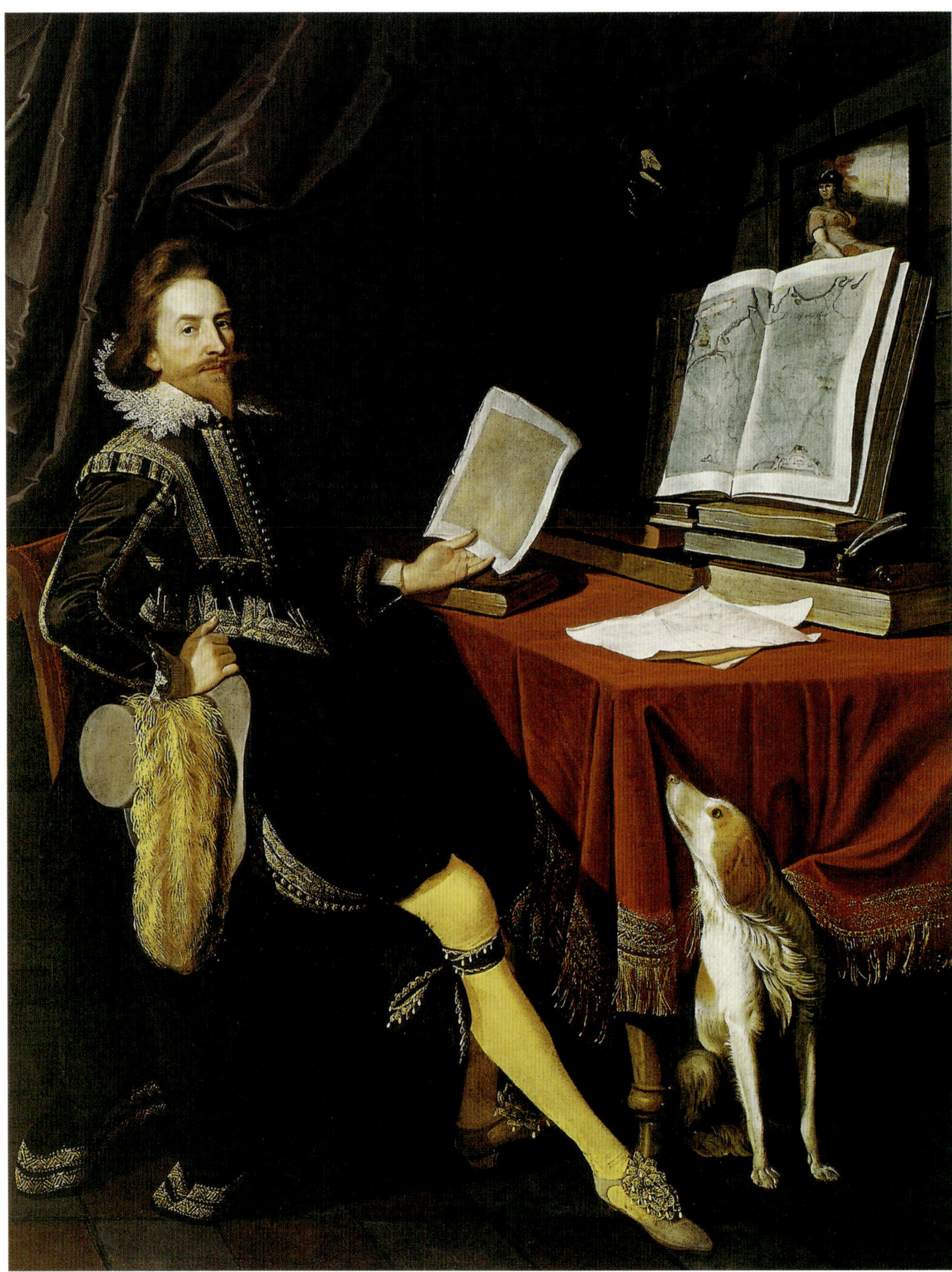

Figure 9

9
Self-Portrait c.1620
Oil on canvas
206.4 × 153.7 cm
Private Collection

painting and the accoutrements of learning (*Scientia*).

On the wall ahead of Bacon is a small painting of, apparently, Pallas Athene, who like the three cookmaids is a full-bosomed figure. It is intriguingly close to a drawing of a female classical figure, possibly Pallas Athene, by Peter Oliver, now in the Ashmolean Museum, Oxford (fig.10) – the same Peter Oliver who was so attached to Nathaniel Bacon's recipe for 'pinke'. Its depicted black frame resembles the ebony one around the surviving landscape signed 'NB' (see fig.4).

Bacon's self-presentation could be compared with that of the Earl of Arundel, seen in Daniel Mytens's celebrated portrait of around 1618 (National Portrait Gallery, on display at Arundel Castle) with his collection of antiquities behind him.[36] Arundel and his wife amassed the foremost collection of art and antiquities of the period, second only to that of Charles I himself. As Earl Marshall and senior representative of the ancient Howard family, Arundel was in charge of the activities of the heralds, which included the investigation, the confirmation and the correct organisation of the system of heraldry and titles. In 1624 Lord Arundel visited Suffolk, and made a specific journey to meet Bacon, who described it in a subsequent

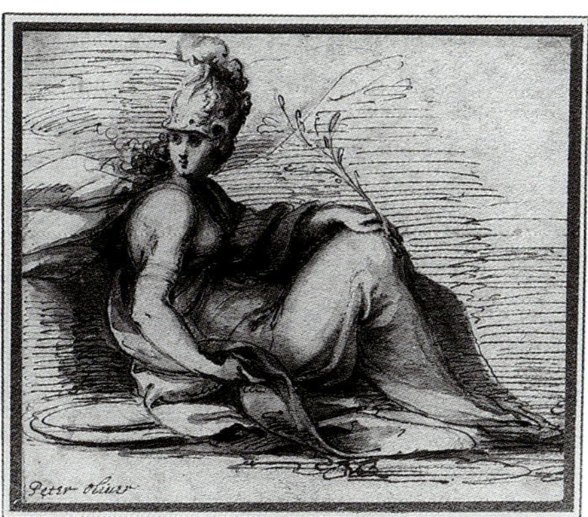

Figure 10

letter. Bacon was not well at the time, but nevertheless 'All the afternoone I waited uppon him about the ruines of the Abby ...'[37] The picture we gain is of two virtuosi discussing archaeological matters, but no doubt this conversation stood Bacon in good stead, when, on the advice of Arundel, he subsequently allowed his name to go forward for admission into the Order of the Bath.

Bacon's funeral certificate, dated 18 December 1627, prepared by Henry Chitting and signed by his wife and executrix Jane, is now at the College of Arms (the headquarters of the heralds) in London.[38] It records the artist's death at Culford Hall on 1 July 1627 and his burial in the chancel in the nearby church, along with his family connections, and it observes that he 'was indued with many excellent virtues besides his endowments of Nature / he was a great lover of all good Artes, and learning and knewe good literature'.

This brief official account of his life set out by the ratifying herald, and the inscription on Bacon's monument, both insist that his own natural gifts – those appropriate to and defining of a gentleman – caused him to embark upon and develop his exercise of the liberal arts. The arts and learning were represented by the classical figure of Pallas Athene who appears in two of his self-portraits. In these Bacon clearly depicts himself with the *sprezzatura* proper to a man of status: 'Nature alone through his experiments with the brush taught him to conquer Nature by art.' It is difficult, however, to believe that Bacon could exercise the technically demanding discipline of oil painting, particularly as it was practised in the early seventeenth century, at such a sophisticated level and in works of such enormous dimensions, without some form of instruction or training, presumably from a professional, probably Netherlandish, whose name is now unknown to us.

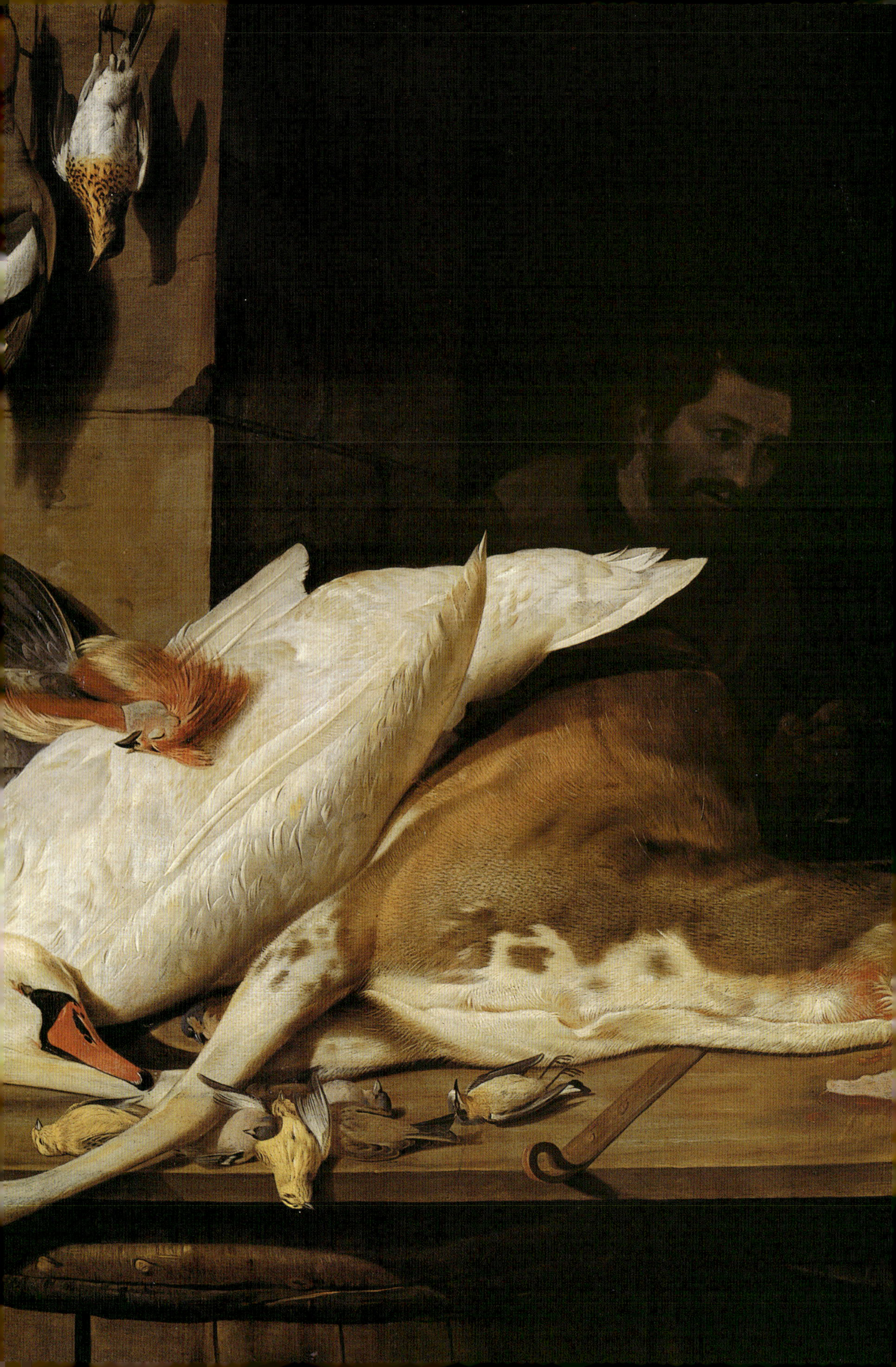

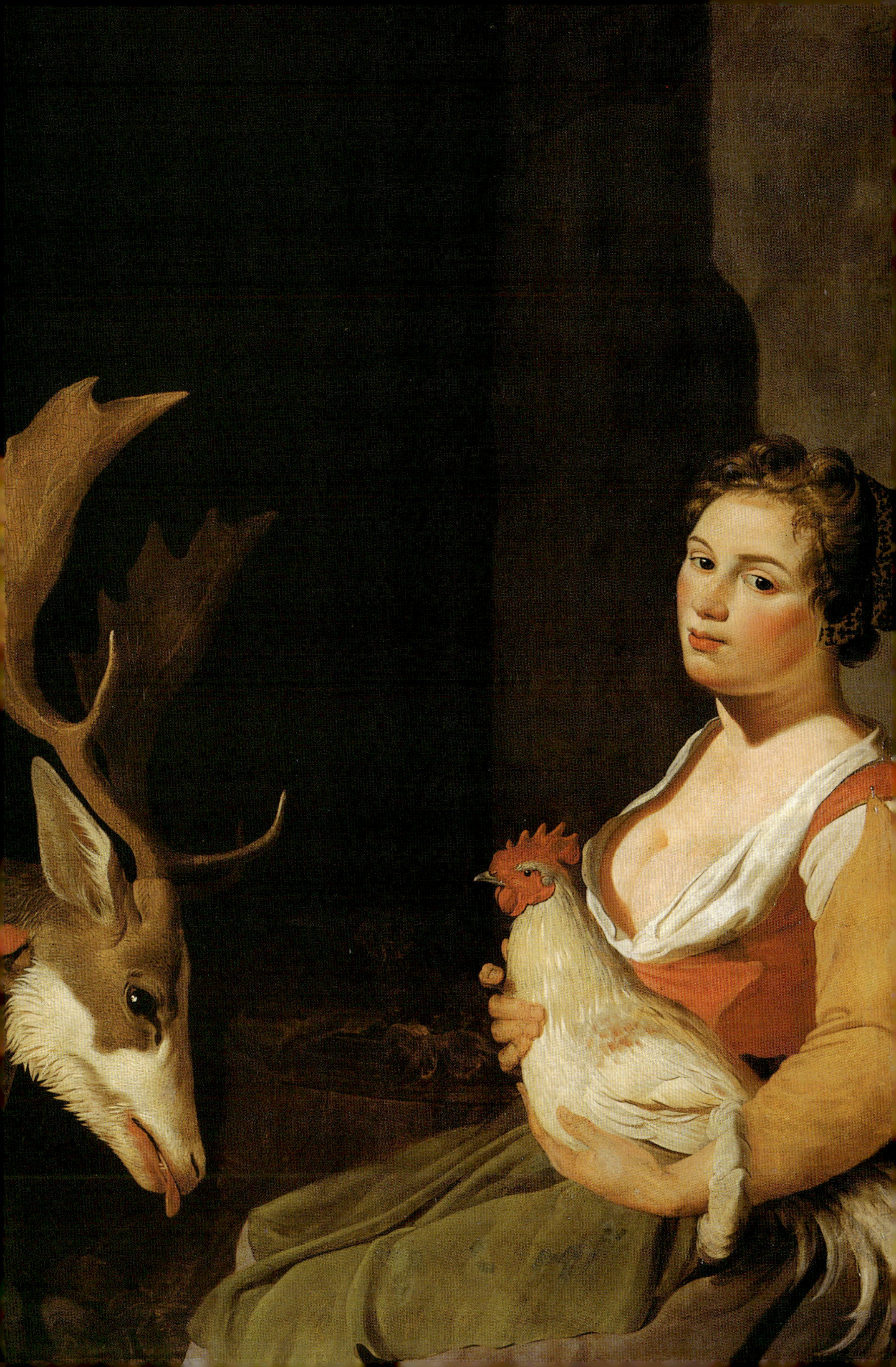

The Cornwallis letters suggest that Bacon travelled a good deal to the Low Countries. The 'kitchen' and 'market scene' subjects, to which Bacon's three *Cookmaids* relate, originated in the Low Countries, where such artists as Pieter Aertsen (1507/8–75) first combined a contemporary kitchen view in the foreground with a depiction of a biblical scene in a room or open area beyond.[39] Aertsen's nephew Joachim Beuckelaer (c.1535–75) – also based in Antwerp – used similar subject matter, developing the still-life area so much that the religious scenes were dispensed with altogether (fig.12).[40] The emphasis is on the dominant figure of the young woman in charge of the produce, with a suggestion that, with her smooth ripe face and figure, she too is part of the delicious and perfect produce laid out for the viewer's gaze. Engravings of such works, particularly those by Aertsen, spread visual knowledge of them more widely.

Another Antwerp artist, Frans Snyders (1579–1657), was a major later exponent of the genre, and it is of course known that Bacon was on his way to Antwerp in 1613. Bacon followed Snyders' lead in producing kitchen scenes that included still lives of game – animals and birds (see figs.1, 11 and 13). Hunting was an aristocratic privilege, so such a scene can be viewed as a celebration of noble status, to be enjoyed by viewers who understood such privileges. Snyders used the dead bodies of glamorous white swans, deer and other birds to demonstrate his skills in rendering a variety of textures. Bacon also grasped the opportunity to show off his ability to paint fur, feathers and flesh on dead and living creatures, as well as, in the Tate painting, the varied surfaces of identifiable fruit and vegetables. This is an expression of the 'experience and observation' that 'made him most knowledgeable in the history of plants', but it also evinces an extremely sensual response to the chosen subject matter. The breasts of all three cookmaids are exposed to an almost unparalleled degree for such works, the cleavage emphasised, the curves echoed among the still-life elements, particularly, in the case of the Tate work, the sliced-open melon.

Although no other English-made examples are known, imported works of this kind had already been recorded in elite British collections. By 1590 Lord Lumley had owned a 'great table of a Dutch woman selling of fruyte'.[41] Most notably, such works are inventoried in the collection of Anne of Denmark, whose circle had included Jane Bacon. At Oatlands Palace in Surrey, prior to Anne's death in 1619, a 'lesser picture of a gardener wth his sonne & daughter selling in ye market mellons, Cabbages, & other hearbes & fruite' was displayed in the Garden Stone Gallery.

In the early eighteenth century George Vertue recorded two further paintings by Bacon, the locations of which are now unknown.[42] Both were of classical subjects – again extremely unusual for a period from which surviving British easel-paintings are almost invariably portraits. One was described as 'Ceres with fruit and flowers', which might just be a Cookmaid type, like the Tate picture. Vertue referred to the other as 'Hercules & Hydra overcome'.

Peter McCullough has recently discovered a reference in the will of the writer William Austin of Southward (c.1587–1633) to 'the picture of the Sunne setting Joseph and Mary made by Sir Nathaniell Bacon' bequeathed to his son James.[43] The location of this work is now unknown, unless it is the Ashmolean *Landscape* (fig.4) in which the tiny figures could perhaps be Joseph and Mary on the Flight into Egypt.

It has been suggested by Margaret Sullivan that Pieter Aertsen devised his cookmaid and market scenes to please an increasingly highly educated section of Netherlandish society, who were purchasing books written in Latin in ever-growing numbers.[44] Classical satires sold well, in a range of affordable editions. Sullivan observes first that Pliny the Elder legitimised low-life painting in his Natural History and, second, that in the writings of such satirists as Juvenal, Horace, Martial and Persius fruit and vegetables, meat and fish, the kitchen and the market place were loaded with moral connotations.

Previous page:
detail of fig.13

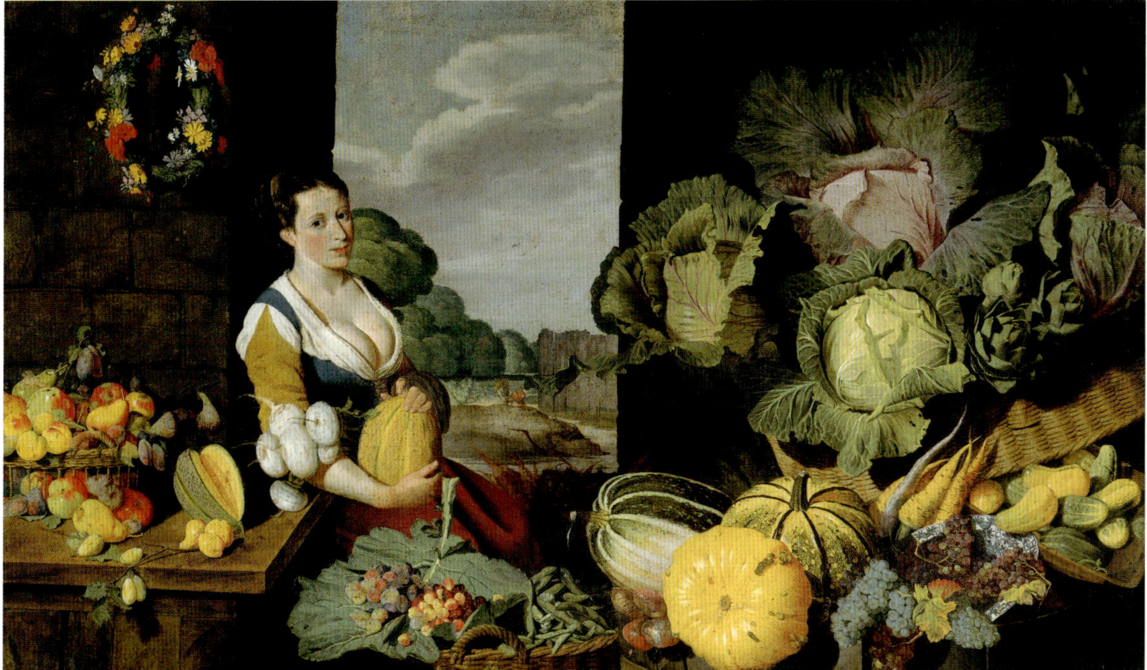

Figure 11

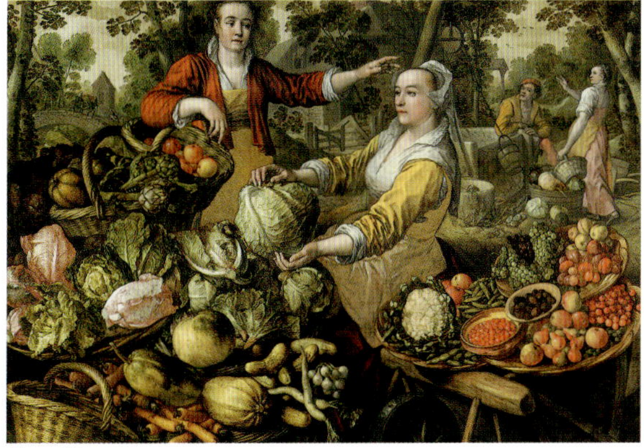

Figure 12

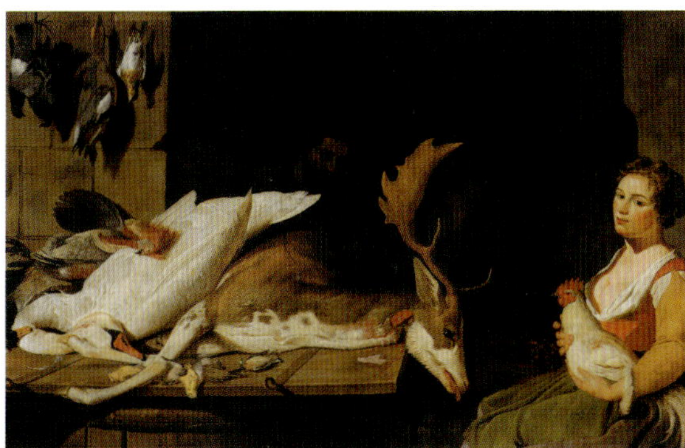

Figure 13

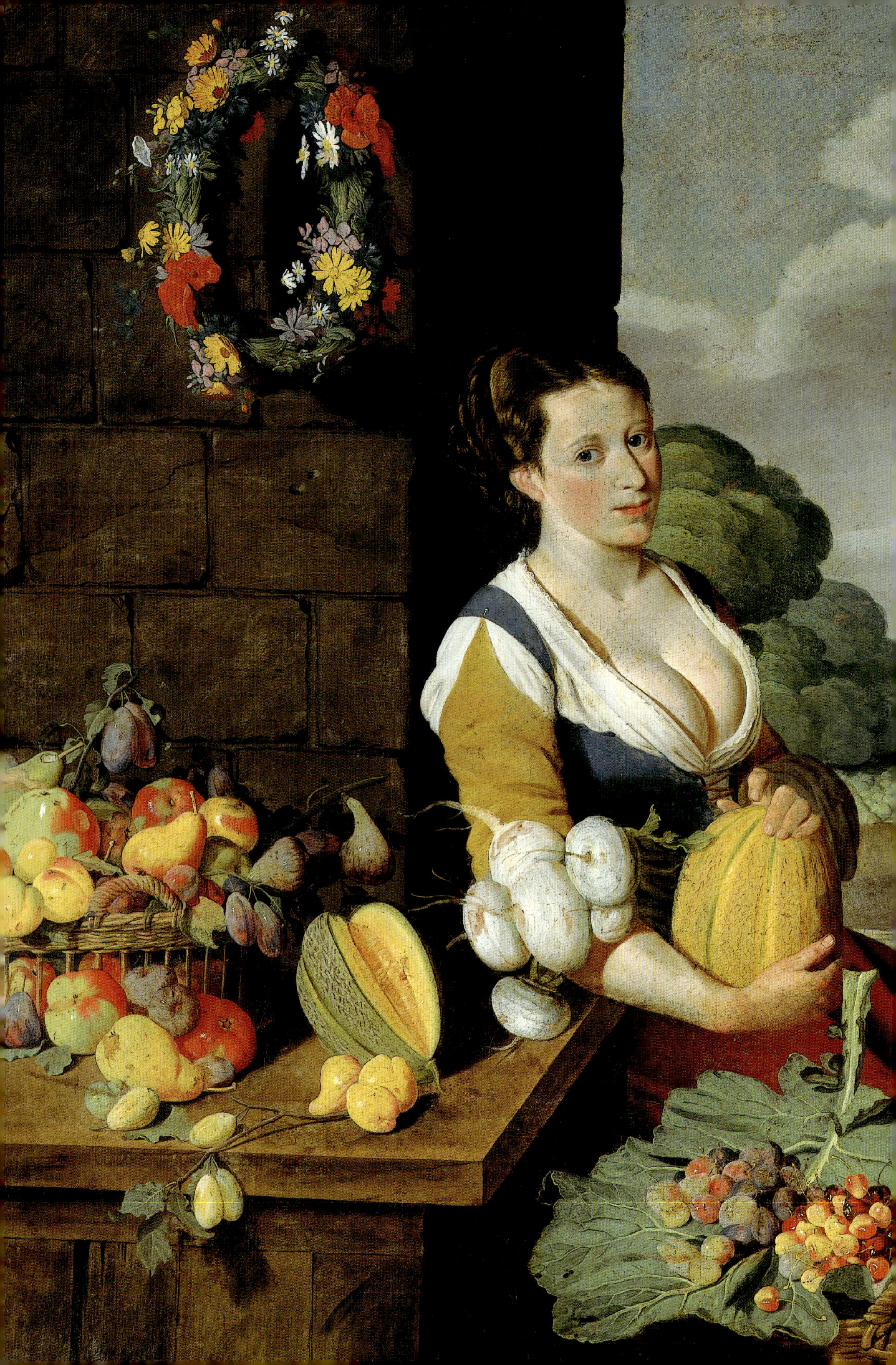

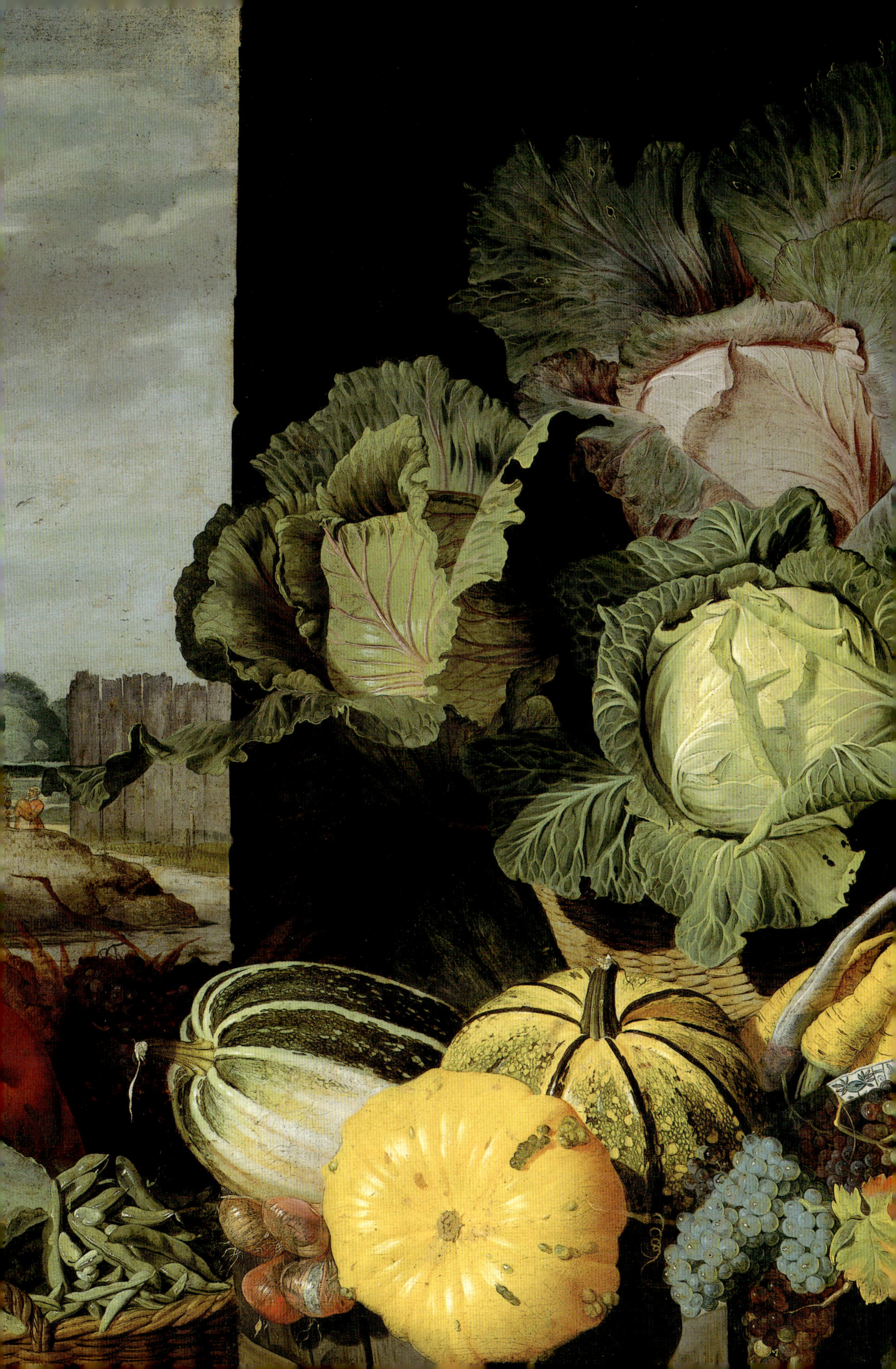

Sir Francis Bacon, Nathaniel's uncle, was not only a natural philosopher and politician but also a horticultural enthusiast. Nathaniel's grandfather and father – and of course Sir Francis – were avid gardeners, laying out, developing and adapting gardens at Gorhambury House, Redgrave Hall and Stiffkey Hall in Norfolk, as well as in properties in and near London.[45] Among the surviving letters to his wife Jane are, as mentioned above, a number from Lucy Harington, Countess of Bedford, celebrated for her own gardens at Twickenham in Surrey (which she had acquired from Sir Francis Bacon) and Moor Park, Herts, no traces of which now remain. So, for instance, from Moor Park Lady Bedford wrote in October 1618 requesting 'som of the little white single rose rootes I saw at Brome, & to chalenge Mr Bacon's promis for som flowers, if about you ther be any extraordinary ones; for I am now very busy furnishing my gardens'. On 6 November she wrote to thank him 'for furnishing me with such helpes for my garden'.[46]

These letters refer to Bacon's other great interest – one that was becoming extremely fashionable in early seventeenth-century Court circles – horticulture. His enthusiasm for, and knowledge of, this subject is highlighted on his funerary monument, in the Latin inscription mentioned above, which stated that 'experience and observation had made him most knowledgeable in the history of plants'. Carved marble swags of leaves and flowers also adorn the monument.

It is known that Bacon grew melons – an exotic fruit given considerable prominence in the Tate picture – in his gardens at Brome. Thomas Meautys, his wife's cousin in London, promised in a letter of June 1626 that 'yf [Nathaniel Bacon] comes to town, I will shew him melons forwarder then his at Broome'.[47] When the gardener John Tradescant the Elder published a plant catalogue in 1634 he included, in the 'Fruits' section, 'Sir Nathaniel Bacons great Peare'.[48] No definite visual record seems to survive of Sir Nathaniel's gardens at Culford and Brome, although extensive gardens (probably laid out by Bacon's stepson Sir Frederick Cornwallis in the 1630s) are shown in Kip and Knyff's engraving of Brome Hall and its grounds, published in 1707 (fig.14).[49] His botanical interests were also implied by Vertue, who said that Bacon 'was in his time much esteem'd for his great skill and knowledge in Art. many of his workes remain being fruits flowers fowls. &c'; some of Bacon's paintings were then still at Culford Hall.[50]

Margaret Sullivan observes that Pieter Aertsen and his Netherlandish followers selected exactly the produce that was given a prominent and moralising role in ancient literature, such as the large and luxuriant cabbage. Pliny had used the giant cabbage known as the 'Tritian', for instance, as a metaphor for luxurious living, but Sullivan suggests that contemporary viewers would recognise the image as a reflection on the moral advantages of living moderately and avoiding excess. Simultaneously, the still-life artist displayed his skill as an illusionist in capturing a diverse range of objects and textures, and meeting the standards set by the painters of antiquity, such as Zeuxis. Classically read patrons would be aware of Pliny's account of the grapes painted by Zeuxis, which were so convincingly depicted that birds flew down and attempted to peck at them; this became a constantly repeated topos in the context of still-life painting. So the artist who made, and the collector who displayed such works – which in the case of Bacon were one and the same – would be demonstrating a sophisticated response to the classical authors, knowledge of whose works was the mark of a gentleman. Rather

Previous page: detail of fig.11

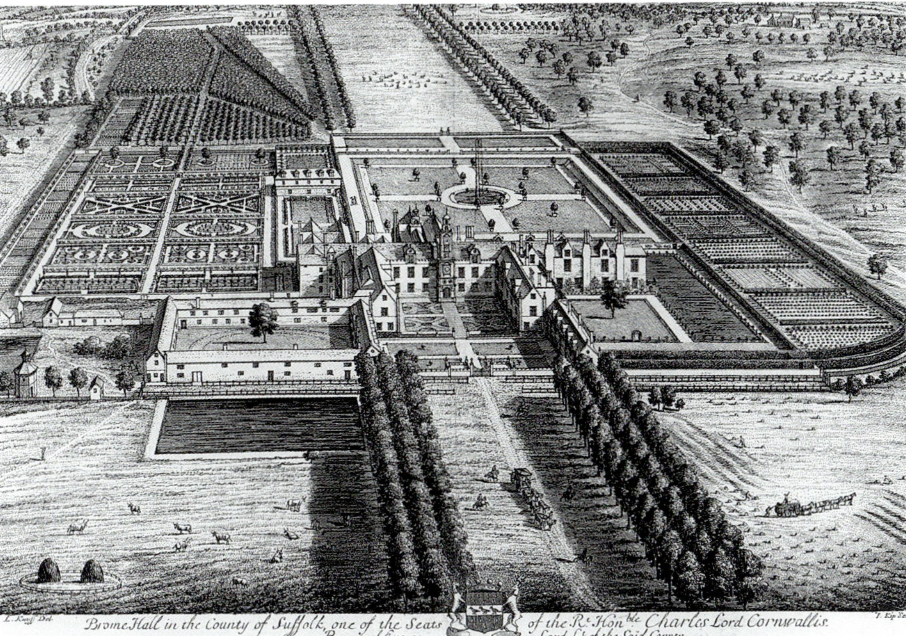

Figure 14

than adopting a moralising purpose, however, Bacon's interest seems to have been in making a visual record of the various items of his constructed still life – one in which the produce in reality would have ripened at differing times of year. It is an expression of the 'experience and observation' that 'made him most knowledgeable in the history of plants'. It also evinces an extremely sensual response to the chosen subject matter.

As stated earlier, Bacon has a surprisingly individual approach to depicting the female cleavage, evident in all his depictions of women (except that of the lady in profile in high status attire, who is thought to be his wife, fig.5, p.11). Contemporary viewers of Bacon's 'cookmaid' pictures are likely to have been well aware of the sexual symbolism inherent in these works. In Netherlandish art birds had unmistakeable sexual connotations, which can be traced back to classical literature. The swelling

forms of melons, gourds and pumpkins were, again, common sexual metaphors in the works of Latin authors. They also conferred sexually charged meaning on the cabbage, and large, round examples were included in Aertsen's kitchen scenes, often sited next to a female subject.[51]

In the Tate painting the bowl filled with grapes in the lower right-hand corner dates from between 1600 and 1620 and is Chinese (fig.15b). It is a type of porcelain made for export for Europe, known as *kraak* ware.[52] Such porcelain was becoming available in London at the start of the seventeenth century and was, for instance, on offer at Lord Salisbury's New Exchange, in The Strand, which was opened by King James I on 11 April 1609. Indeed, on his death in 1612 the earl himself owned at least sixty pieces of porcelain.[53] Imitations of *kraak* ware were also made in the Netherlands and exported.

14
Brome Hall, Suffolk
in Leonard Knyff
and Joannes Kip
Britannia Illustrata
(1707)

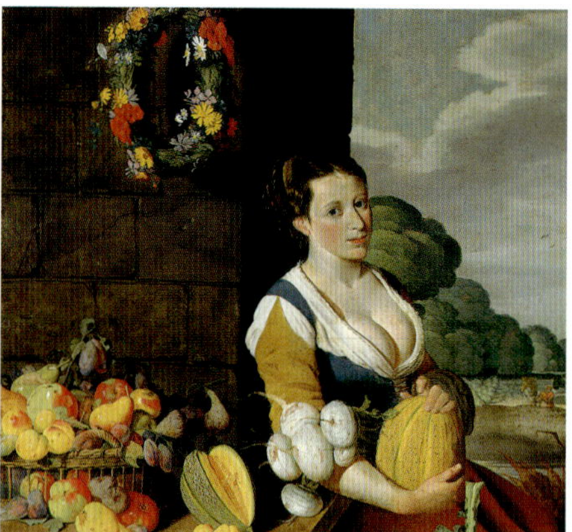

Figure 15a

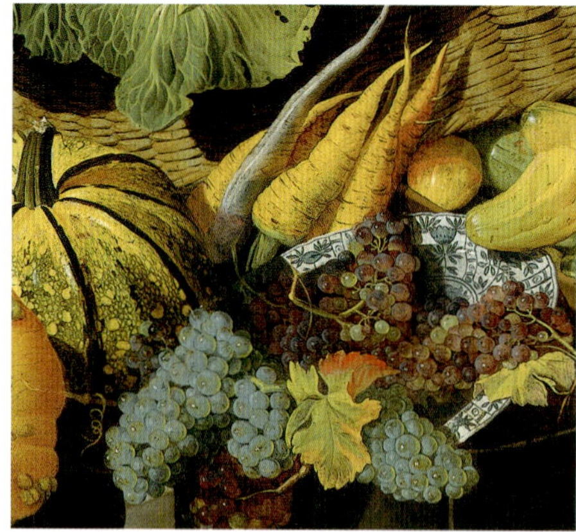

Figure 15b

The particular plant varieties that Bacon depicted in the Tate painting suggest that he may also have been pursuing his horticultural interests in the Low Countries. Dr Barrie Juniper has made a close analysis of the produce depicted,[54] some of which had originated in the New World, such as, on the right of the picture, marrows (*Cucurbita pepo*), squashes (*Cucurbita mixta* and *C. maxima*), pumpkins (*C. moschata*) and what may be *C. maxima* cv. 'Turbaniformis' – the ornamental 'Turk's Cap' gourd – tucked in at the lower rim of the large basket. The curved cucurbits to the right, in the gardening trug, may be the forerunners of present-day 'Summer Crookneck'. Also in this group may appear early versions of a cucumber (*Cucumis sativus*) and gherkin (*Cucumis anguria*), which are Cucurbitaceae too, but Old World selections. The other striking New World item may be the bunch of runner beans (*Phaseolus coccineus*) in the double-handled basket in the centre foreground. These would appear to be mixed up with broad beans (*Vicia faba*) at the back, along with some peas (*Pisum sativum*) hanging over the rim at the front. The last two are both from the Old World, but Bacon has here assembled an international collection of important Leguminosae.

Most of the rest of the cornucopia are Old World, but some are given greater prominence than others. The black grapes (*Vitis vinifera*) in the imported *kraak* dish would have had their origins in the Far East, but the light-coloured grapes might be a variety of *Vitis labrusca*, fairly recently brought in from North America. The yellow and red segmentation of the vine leaves in the right foreground may indicate a virus infection.[55] But Bacon obviously gives pride of place to the melon (*Cucumis melo* subsp. *melo*), two cultivars of which are shown.

Another prestigious item is the bunch of white turnips (*Brassica rapa*) at the cookmaid's right elbow (fig.15a). If Bacon grew them in Suffolk, he was almost certainly importing either the plants or the seeds from the Low Countries. Run-of-the-mill fruit and vegetables in the picture get less attention. There are brown-skinned onions (*Allium cepa*) originally from the Middle East. The foremost of these onions, with its hint of blue coloration, may possibly be infected with *Botrytis* mould, which causes storage rots. Cherries, cherry-plums and mirabelles ('myrobolan' plums, *Prunus cerasifera*) nestle on a cabbage leaf in the foreground. Quinces (*Cydonia oblonga*) rest on the corner of the table along with

15a/15b
Cookmaid with Still Life of Vegetables and Fruit
*c.*1620–5
(details of fig.11)

greengages, plums, black and white cultivars of figs and, in the basket, peaches, plums, pears and perhaps two varieties of apple (*Malus pumila* from central Asia).

To the right, and in the background, can be seen immense cabbages (*Brassica oleracea* subsp. *capitata*) in green, white and blue forms. These may be identified as 'kraut' cabbages, giant farm selections and often preserved in brine or vinegar for the winter. The swollen veins of some of the cabbage leaves may also indicate a virus infection. Rows of these huge cabbages can be seen in the garden in the background, behind a rough vertical fence of planks. Nestling between the krauts, right centre, are globe artichokes (*Cynara scolymus*). Also in the right-centre, but to the front, are four root vegetables. The thin light brown root is probably a skirret (*Sium sisarum*), also from central Asia. The other three roots at first sight look like parsnips (*Pastinaca sativa*) but are more probably yellow carrots (*Daucus carota* subsp. *sativus*).

Hanging on the wall behind the maid is a garland, principally of meadow flowers, but perhaps containing a few garden cultivars as well. Like the fruits and vegetables, these flowers must have been painted over at least a six-week period. But the later blooms are perhaps typical of the beginning of the hay harvest near the end of July. Reading from twelve o'clock clockwise, are stinking chamomile (*Anthemis cotula*) or corn chamomile (*Anthemis arvensis*), lady's smock (*Cardamine pratensis*), field poppy (*Papaver rhoeas*), ox-eye daisy (*Leucanthemum vulgare*) or wild chamomile (*Matricaria restita*), lady's smock again, corn marigold (*Chrysanthemum segetum*), greater stitchwort (*Stellaria holostea*), an unidentified marigold (*Calendula*, possibly a 'garden escape'), field poppy again, chicory (*Cichorium intybus*), yellow ox-eye or tansy (*Chrysanthemum vulgare* or *Tanacetum vulgare*), field bindweed (*Convolvulus arvensis*) or hedge bindweed (*Calystegia sepium*), charlock/wild mustard (*Sinapis arvensis*) and the garden marigold again.

Dr Juniper's research indicates the fidelity to nature that Bacon set out to achieve in his still-life paintings, particularly in the Tate work, and it helps to substantiate the horticultural claims made for Bacon both on his funerary monument and by contemporary and subsequent commentators.

Surviving paintings by Bacon are few in number, but it is distinctly possible that further examples may yet be discovered and identified. The quality of Bacon's painting is so high, his style so un-British, and much of his subject-matter so unexpected, that his works are not necessarily easily recognised. The chance survival of some of his personal correspondence with his wife opens a window onto his personal life and attitudes in a way that is unprecedented for a British artist. His high social status was unusual for a painter in England, but he was active during a period at which an informed interest in the visual arts was becoming a significant indicator of a gentleman. All these elements combine to make him a unique figure in the story of art in Britain.

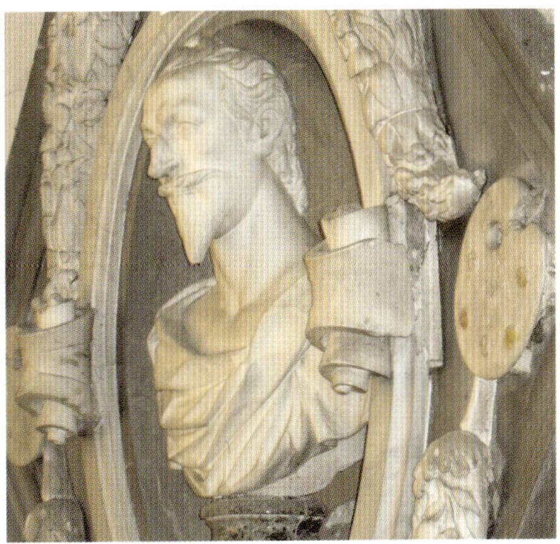

Figure 16

1 See Karen Hearn, 'Sir Nathaniel Bacon I: Horticulturalist and Artist', *British Art Journal*, vol.1, no.2, Spring 2000, pp.13–15. Some material from that paper is reproduced here with permission of the editor of the *British Art Journal*. 'Nathaniel' was, and continues to be, a first name much used in the Bacon family and past writers have sometimes confused the painter with, for instance, his uncle, Sir Nathaniel Bacon of Stiffkey (1546–1615).

2 Adam White, 'Biographical Dictionary of London Tomb Sculptors *c*.1560–*c*.1660', *Walpole Society*, LXI, 1999; and Hearn 2000, p.15.

3 Some early accounts refer also to representations of brushes on the monument, e.g. George Vertue, 'Note Books', IV, *Walpole Society*, Oxford 1935–6, pp.161–2. Truncated marble fragments that protrude from underneath the carved palettes may be the last traces of these; I am grateful to Marcus Leith and Andrew Dunkley, whose photographic lighting revealed these.

4 Translation by Dr Keith Cunliffe. The original reads: 'VIATOR / SPECTA / NATHANIELIS BACONII AD BALNEVM REGALE / TORQVATI EQVITIS / EFFIGIES / HAEC EST / QVEM QVVM VSVS ET OBSERVATIO IN / STIRPIVM HISTORIA SAPIENTISSIMVM /FECERANT, EVNDEM, EN MIRVM, IM / IISDEM PENECILLO EXPRIMENDIS / SOLA NATVRA DOCVIT / ARTE NATVRAM VINCERE. / SAT DEBES OCVLIS / VALE.' Bacon's will, dated 8 June 1627, survives in the National Archives (PROB/ 11/152). Apart from some land for his two young daughters, all his property went to his wife Jane. The witnesses were: Henry Chitting, William Greenhill, Robert Morse and John Fenn.

5 Braybrooke 1842 (see note 6 below), pp.xlix–xlx.

6 On deposit at Essex Record Office (Braybrooke MSS), D/Dby C 15–18. Edited and privately published by Lord Braybrooke as *The Private Correspondence of Jane Lady Cornwallis*, Audley End 1842. A recent edition, edited by Joanna Moody as *The Private Correspondence of Jane Lady Cornwallis (1613–1644)*, Madison and London, was published in 2003.

7 See Karen Hearn, 'A Question of Judgement: Lucy Harington, Countess of Bedford, as Art Patron and Collector' in *The Evolution of English Collecting*, ed. Edward Chaney, New Haven and London 2003, pp.221–39.

8 Braybrooke 1842, p.11, Moody 2003, p.67.

9 See Hearn 2000, p.15, note 24.

10 Braybrooke 1842, pp.94–5; in 1659 Richard Symonds was to refer to 'Fenn the Liegois in Purpoole Lane' in London, who sold artists' materials – see Hearn 2000, p.15, note 29.

11 Herts Record Office, Gorhambury IX.D.54.

12 Hearn 2000, p.15, note 13.

13 Ibid. A watercolour of the 1830s by Nicholas Condy (*c*.1793–1857) shows that at that date it and another rather similar still life of game and birds (whereabouts now unknown) hung high in the entrance hall at Antony House, Cornwall (reproduced in Oliver Garnett, *Images*, London 1995, p.95); any of a number of the works listed in an Antony inventory of 1792 could have been these (I am grateful to Christine North for checking the Antony muniments for references).

14 Tate acc. no.T06995, oil on canvas, 151 x 246.7 cm purchased with assistance from the National Art Collections Fund, 1995. The early history of this painting is unknown. It was at Roddam Hall, near Alnwick, by at least the early twentieth century from whence it descended to the late Mr David Holderness-Roddam; by whom it was sold at Christie's 9 July 1993 (lot 9, as by Nicholaes van Heussen), where bought by the late Mr Ronald Lee, by whom sold to Tate 1995. See Hearn 2000, and Barrie Juniper, 'Sir Nathaniel Bacon II: The Vegetable World', *British Art Journal*, vol.1, no.2, Spring 2000, pp.16–18.

15 The next to do so was Alexander Marshall (*c*.1610–20 – 1682) amateur painter of flowers and fruits, of independent means, who experimented with pigments that he extracted from plant parts, see *The Dictionary of Art*, ed. Jane Turner, vol.20, 1996, pp.476–7.

16 John Tradescant, *Musaeum Tradescantianum: or a collection of rarities ...*, London, 1656, p.40: the list of 'Principall Benefactors to the precedent Collection' includes both 'Sir Nathanael Bacon' and his brother Sir Butts Bacon, p.180. For the painting, see Karen Hearn (ed.), *Dynasties: Painting in Tudor and Jacobean England 1530–1630*, Tate 1995, p.116, no.114; Kim Sloan, '*A Noble Art*': Amateur Artists and Drawing Masters *c*.1600–1800, London 2000, 40–1, 85.

17 Hearn 2000, p.15, note 30. A full-length portrait of a blonde lady in a classical garden, from the late 1620s, by George Geldorp (*c*.1595–1665), in the collection of Lord Braybrooke, bears a later inscription 'Jane Lady Bacon', bottom right (reproduced Moody, facing title page).

18 A copy of this work was formerly at Gillingham Hall in Norfolk, and is now in a private collection.

19 Reproduced Sotheby sale catalogue, 14 July 1993 (17), but withdrawn prior to the sale.

20 Hearn 1995, p.120, no.67.

21 Hearn 1995, pp.125–6, no.73. See Nicholas Hilliard, 'A Treatise Concerning the Arte of Limning', MS Laing III, 174, Edinburgh University, published as Thornton, R.K.R., and Cain, T.G.S. (eds.), *The Art of Limning*, Ashington and Manchester 1981.

22 Hearn 1995, p.130, no.77.

23 Hearn 1995, pp.107–8, no.57.

24 Henry Peacham, *The Compleat Gentleman*, London 1622, pp.106–7.

25 See Ann Bermingham, *Learning to Draw: Studies in the Cultural History of a Polite and Useful Art*, New Haven and London 2000, chapter 2, especially p.35.

26 His brother Sir Edmund (1566–1649) had a laboratory at Redgrave and conducted experiments of various kinds. Sir Edmund's friend and kinsman Sir Henry Wotton noted the technique that he had developed for tinting and colouring stones (see J.T. Cliffe, *The World of the Country House in Seventeenth-Century England*, New Haven and London 1999, p.175). In his will dated 1645 Sir Edmund bequeathed items from his 'Labouratory' thus: 'a great grinding stone of Purfore [i.e. porphyry] with the Miller [i.e. muller] ... alsoe my two perspectives of St Marke' to the Revd John Craddock (father of the painter Mary Beale); to his nephew Butts Bacon 'my great Limbeck [alembic] in the Labouratory ...'; and to Richard Hinchler 'my great Herball bound in Leather composed by Mr John Parkinson Apothecary' (British Library Add. Mss 39,218).

27 The recipe, which survives in a number of manuscript copies, is published in Edward Norgate, *Miniatura or the Art of Limning*, ed. Jeffrey M. Muller and Jim Murrell, New Haven and London 1997, p.99: *Genistella tinctoria* (Gerard, *Herball*, 1597) now *Genista tinctoria*.

28 Ibid. p.70. In addition, the unidentified author of the manuscript BL Harleian 6676, after transcribing the recipe (fol.79–80), explained that 'This did Sr Nathaniell Bacon teach me and I proved it, and found it far better then any I could buy both for Limning & painting [i.e. for painting in both water-bound and oil-bound paints].'

29 See Jo Kirby, 'Sir Nathaniel Bacon's "Pinke"', in *Dyes in History and Archaeology 19*, ed. Jo Kirby, 2003, p.42. No other work by Bacon has yet had paint samples taken and examined in such detail.

30 British Library, Add. MS 12,461, fols 45v–46r, see M. Kirby Talley, *Portrait Painting in England: Studies in the Technical Literature before 1700*, London 1981, p.49, and Jo Kirby, 'The painter's trade in the seventeenth century', in *National Gallery Technical Bulletin* 20, 1999, p.48, note 176.

31 Braybrooke 1842, p.51: Moody 2003, p.90.

32 Braybrooke 1842, pp.184–5; Moody 2003, pp.175–6. It has been suggested that *The Supper at Emmaus* 1612, by the Haarlem painter Cornelius Engelsz, formerly at a Bacon family property, Gillingham Hall in Norfolk, and recently acquired by the Castle Museum, Norwich, may have been brought to England by Bacon, though there is no documentary evidence for this (personal communication, Andrew Moore, 2005).

33 Cited in Felicity Heal and Clive Holmes, '*Prudentia ultra sexum*: Lady Jane Bacon and the Management of her Families', in *Protestant Identities: Religion, Society, and Self-Fashioning in Post-Reformation England*, ed. Muriel C. McClendon *et al.*, Stanford 1999, p.114.

34 As suggested by Sir Oliver Millar in Gervase Jackson-Stops (ed.), *The Treasure Houses of Britain*, exh. cat., National Gallery of Art, Washington 1985, p.150.

35 I am grateful to Peter Barber for identifying this map and observing that Bacon has even reproduced the double-headed Imperial eagle with Habsburg arms on its breast, lower left. He notes that this map had last appeared in an Ortelius atlas in 1602.

36 See Hearn 1995, p.208, no.140.

37 Braybrooke 1842, pp.91–2; Moody 2003, pp.110–11.

38 College of Arms I 23ff 18 and 18v. I am grateful to Timothy Duke, Chester Herald, for enabling me to examine this. The certificate continues: 'He dyed of a long languishing desease, too soone, in the full strength of his yeares most religiously as he lived beloved of all in his own County so lamented in his departure of all that knew him.' Mr Duke observes that Bacon's funeral certificate is unusually long and expressive. The herald Henry Chitting (1580–1638) was a Suffolk man with strong links with the Bacon family (see H.C.G. Matthew and Brian Harrison (eds.), *Oxford Dictionary of National Biography*, Oxford 2004, vol. 11: entry on 'Henry Chitting', p.498); he witnessed the artist's will, and Jane Bacon's inventory (see p.32 of this book) includes a portrait of 'Mr Chittinge'.

39 Josua Bruyn has recently suggested that Aertsen's little-documented other nephew, Huybrecht Beuckelaer, may be identified with the artist previously known in England simply as 'Hubbard', to whom payments were made during the 1580s by various English clients. These included the Earl of Leicester, who in 1583 owned 'A device made by Hubbard on clothe

of a Butchar and a Maide buying meate' (Kent Record Office, Dudley Papers VII). No surviving English works by 'Hubbard' have been identified with certainty. Dr Bruyn's researches suggest that he may have learnt to paint such subject matter in Antwerp from his uncle; see Josua Bruyn, 'Hubert (Huybert) Beuckelaer, an Antwerp portrait painter and his English patron, the Earl of Leicester', in *Dutch and Flemish Artists in Britain 1550–1800*, ed. Juliette Roding *et al.*, Leiden 2003, pp.85–112.

40 See Lorne Campbell, 'Beuckelaer's *The Four Elements*: Four masterpieces by a neglected genius', *Apollo*, Feb. 2002, pp.40–6.

41 See Hearn 1995, p.220, no.148.

42 'Two large pictures at Redgrave Hall in Suffolke. by Nath Bacon. one Ceres with fruit & flowers. the other Hercules & Hydra overcome', owned by 'Mr Rowland Holt'. George Vertue, 'Note Books', II, *Walpole Society*, Oxford 1931–3, p.67. They must already have moved out of the possession of Bacon's descendants, having presumably been sold, along with Redgrave itself, by Sir Robert Bacon, 5th Bart., to Chief Justice Sir John Holt (1642–1709) at the turn of the seventeenth century.

43 Personal communication, June 2005; National Archives (PROB/11/165).

44 Margaret A. Sullivan, 'Aertsen's Kitchen and Market Scenes: Audience and Innovation in Northern Art', *Art Bulletin*, LXXXI, no.2, June 1999, pp.236–66.

45 See Hassell Smith, 'The Gardens of Sir Nicholas and Sir Francis Bacon: an enigma resolved and a mind explored', in Anthony Fletcher and Peter Roberts (ed.), *Religion, Culture and Society in Early Modern Britain*, Cambridge 1994, pp.125–60, and Paula Henderson *The Tudor House and Garden*, New Haven and London 2005, pp.132–3, 151–2.

46 Braybrooke 1842, pp.57, 58; Moody 2003, pp.93–4; Hearn 2000, p.14.

47 Braybrooke 1842, p.164; Moody 2003, pp.153–4.

48 See *The John Tradescants*, Prudence Leith-Ross, London 1984, p.222 (I am indebted for this reference to Hassell Smith).

49 See John Harris and Gervase Jackson-Stops (eds.), *Britannia Illustrata: Knyff and Kip*, Bungay 1984, p.183, repr. pp.96–7.

50 Vertue 1935–6, pp.161–2.

51 See Sullivan 1999, p.258.

52 Identified by Rose Kerr, Victoria and Albert Museum. I am grateful also to Jessica Harrison-Hall, Stacey Peirson and Ann Tozer for advice and assistance.

53 See James Knowles, 'Cecil's shopping centre', *Times Literary Supplement*, 7 February 1997, pp.14–15 (I owe this reference to the late Leslie Parris).

Further Reading

Lord Braybrooke, *The Private Correspondence of Jane Lady Cornwallis*, Audley End 1842.

Bernard Denvir, 'Sir Nathaniel Bacon', *Connoisseur*, vol.156, May 1964, pp.116–19.

Felicity Heal and Clive Holmes, '*Prudentia ultra sexum*: Lady Jane Bacon and the Management of her Families', in *Protestant Identities: Religion, Society, and Self-Fashioning in Post-Reformation England*, ed. Muriel C. McClendon *et al.*, Stanford 1999, pp.100–24.

Karen Hearn (ed.), *Dynasties: Painting in Tudor and Jacobean England 1530–1630*, exh. cat., Tate 1995.

Karen Hearn, 'Sir Nathaniel Bacon I: Horticulturalist and Artist', *British Art Journal*, vol.1, no.2, Spring 2000, pp.13–15.

Barrie Juniper, 'Sir Nathaniel Bacon II: The Vegetable World', *British Art Journal*, vol.1, no.2, Spring 2000, pp.16–18.

Jo Kirby, 'Sir Nathaniel Bacon's "Pinke"', in *Dyes in History and Archaeology 19*, ed. Jo Kirby, 2003, pp.37–50.

M. Kirby Talley, *Portrait Painting in England: Studies in the Technical Literature before 1700*, 1981.

H.C.G. Matthew and Brian Harrison (eds.), *Oxford Dictionary of National Biography*, Oxford 2004, vol.3: entry on 'Jane Bacon' by Joanna Moody, pp.153–4; and entry on 'Sir Nathaniel Bacon' by Karen Hearn, pp.160–1.

Joanna Moody, *The Private Correspondence of Jane Lady Cornwallis (1613–1644)*, Madison and London 2003.

Edward Norgate, *Miniatura or the Art of Limning*, ed. Jeffrey M. Muller and Jim Murrell, New Haven and London 1997.

Clive Paine (ed.), *The Culford Estate 1780–1935*, Lavenham 1993

Henry Peacham, *The Compleat Gentleman*, London 1622, pp.106–7.

Kim Sloan, *'A Noble Art': Amateur Artists and Drawing Masters c.1600–1800*, London 2000, pp.40–1, 85.

Gertrude Storey, 'Culford Hall', in *People and Places*, Lavenham 1973.

George Vertue, 'Note Books', I–VI, *Walpole Society*, vols.18, 20, 22, 24, 26, 30, Oxford 1930–55.

Photographic Credits

All photographs were supplied courtesy of the credited owner of the work with whom rests the photographic copyright, except where outlined below:

Tate Photography: Andrew Dunkley/ Dave Lambert/Marcus Leith/ Rodney Tidnam, figs.1, 2, 5, 6, 9, 11, 13, 16

Acknowledgements

The author would like to thank the following for their advice and help over years of research into Sir Nathaniel Bacon:

Sir Nicholas and Lady Bacon, Dr Peter Barber, Rosie Bass, John Blatchly, Susan Bracken, Dr Christopher Brown, Dr Keith Cunliffe, Timothy Duke (Chester Herald), Dr Brent Elliott, Mrs Susan Flood (Herts Archives and Local Studies), Dr Claire Gapper, Robert Harding, Richard Harris (Essex Record Office), Professor Elizabeth Honig, Dr Barrie Juniper, Dr Peter McCullough, Sir Oliver Millar, the late Leslie Parris, Karen Peters (The Royal Society), Paul Petzold, Robin Simon, Professor A. Hassell Smith, The Earl of Verulam, Dr Adam White, Dr Timothy Wilks, Renate Woudhuysen-Keller.

Very special acknowledgement is owed to the former Keeper of the British Collection at Tate, Andrew Wilton, who championed the Tate acquisition of Bacon's *Cookmaid with Still Life of Vegetables and Fruit*; also to The Art Fund's panel of Expert Advisors who supported it.

Karen Hearn

An Inventory of the Pictures belonginge to Culford.

Sir Nathaniel Bacon's widow Jane died in 1659. As specified in her will, an inventory was made on 28 June that year of all the goods at Culford Hall which, along with its contents, she bequeathed to her son Nicholas Bacon Esq. for his lifetime. Comprising eleven vellum sheets, its first page (now the back sheet, since the pages have been bound from back to front) is endorsed 'An Inventory of all the goods and household stuff belonging to Culford 1659.'[1] The present-day front sheet is a list of the pictures then at Culford. Some had been added in the thirty or so years following the artist's death, but many must have been owned by him. Jane's will itself, dated 28 March 1659, alluded to 'All my pictures which were the said Sir Nathaniell Bacon's my late husband and all other my pictures at Culford ...'[2] The inventory specifically refers to a group of ten large paintings as being by Nathaniel himself.

This front page of the inventory, previously unpublished, is here transcribed (right). Where possible, identities for the subjects of the portraits listed are proposed in footnotes.

In the inward Parlour.
1 Queene Annes[3] Pictures
2 The Ladie Bacon yᵉ Younger [4]
3 The Ladie Bacon theldᵉʳ
4 The Ladie Bath [6]
5 The Lord Mountagues daughter [7]
6 Mris Frances Gaudy. [8]
7 Mris Eliz:Walldgrave [9]
8 Mris Bacon
9 Mrs Anne Bacon
10 Mr Butts [10]
11 Mʳˢ Phillip Colbye [11]
12 Mʳˢ Iem: Waldgrave [12]
13 Mʳˢ Butts.
14 Sir Butts Bacon. [13]
15 Sʳ Edmund Bacon. [14]
16 Mʳ Nicholas Bacon th'oldʳ.
17 Mʳ Parr [15]
18 Mʳ Greenhill [16]
19 Mʳ Chittinge [17]
20 Mʳ Glovett
21 Sʳ Francis Vere [18]
22 Sʳ Edmund Bacon. [19]
23 Mr Simons.

Sixe peeces with Flowers little
   and great
Eighteen Lantsheps little & great
Five peeces with Shipps & tempests
Two Night peeces.
Hagar and the Angell
The little Brasse peece
Herod & Herodias
The Centaures
The peece with the Owle
   on the baskett
The peece with rootes & cabbage
The peece wᵗʰ the hooping birds
The distruction of Sodome
The Little round Mapp
St George.
The Mapp over the Chimney

Peeces in the great Parlor
The Paper peece.
Moses striking the Rocke
One large Mapp of the world
One Lantschape
The Hawke over the dore
Paurett [20] & grapes
The doggs,
Sᵗ Sebastian
Two, Sybbills
Five peeces of Butts famalye [21]
Two peeces of the Lord
   keep[er]Bacon [22]
One of Sʳ Nichas Bacon. [23]
The Ladie Drury [24]
Duck Frokin & a Fansye

More peeces suice hunge up in the great Parlor [videlt]
Sᵗ Hirom
Mr Gilberds
Mr Slaike
Shillinge the Gardner [25]

On the great Stayere and in the Gallery
Ten, Great peeces in Wainscoate of fish and fowle &c done by
   Sr: Nath:Bacon, [26]
The picture of the two Lyons
The peece wᵗʰ two deeres heads
   and Haunch.
The peece with the badgers
The Cupboard of plate.

Notes to the Inventory

1 On deposit at Herts Archives and Local Studies, Gorhambury IX.D.54.
2 National Archives, PROB/11/300, folio 9.
3 Anne of Denmark (1574–1619), wife of James I of England and Scotland, whom Jane Bacon had attended at Court.
4 Presumably Jane Bacon herself.
5 Presumably Sir Nathaniel's mother, Anne Bacon, died 1616.
6 Mary Cornwallis, Countess of Bath, died 1627, sister to Jane's first husband.
7 Perhaps a daughter of Edward, 1st Baron Montagu of Boughton (*c.*1562–1644), cousin of Jane's good friend, Lucy, Countess of Bedford.
8 In 1595 the artist's sister Dorothy (*c.*1574–1621) wed as her first husband Sir Bassingborne Gawdy of West Harling, Norfolk; their daughter Frances (1604–26) remained unmarried.
9 Perhaps a niece of the artist (see note 12, below).
10 The artist's mother Anne was daughter and heir to Edmund Butts of Barrow, Norfolk. The family fortune had been made by her grandfather, Sir William Butts (*c.*1483–1545), physician to Henry VIII (who with his wife Margaret, née Bacon, had been painted by Hans Holbein II; both portraits are now in the Isabella Stewart Gardner Museum, Boston). Anne also inherited the property of her two uncles, Sir William Butts of Thornage, Norfolk, and Thomas Butts (died 1593) of Great Ryburgh in Norfolk who, Hassell Smith suggests, may be depicted here.
11 In 1609 the artist's sister Dorothy (see note 8 above) married secondly Philip Coleby, whom the artist described in a letter of 1624 as 'my brother Coleby'.
12 The artist's sister Jemimah married Sir William Waldegrave of Smallbridge in Suffolk.
13 Brother of the artist; a head-and-shoulders portrait survives at Raveningham Hall.
14 Eldest brother of the artist.
15 Rev. Elnathan Parr (1577–1622), religious author, rector of Palgrave in Suffolk and religious adviser to Jane Bacon (Oxford DNB, vol.42, pp.840–1).
16 William Greenhill (1597/8–1671) puritan clergyman who became rector of Oakley in Suffolk in 1628 (see *Oxford DNB*, vol.23, pp.601–3). He witnessed the artist's will in 1627.
17 Henry Chitting (1580–1638) was a herald. He witnessed the artist's will, officiated at his funeral (and at that of his father) and had close links with the Bacon family (see Oxford DNB, vol. 11, p.498). The only known surviving portrait of him is a head and shoulders on panel (now College of Arms, London).
18 Sir Francis Vere (1560/1–1609), soldier and diplomat, commanded English regiments in the Low Countries on the Protestant side: the artist's brother-in-law Sir Robert Drury served there with him in 1597 and 1598.
19 See note 14 above.
20 Presumably 'parrot'.
21 See note 10 above. The artist's great-uncle Thomas Butts is known to have owned a group of five portraits of radical clergymen (personal communication from Hassell Smith, June 2005).
22 Grandfather of the artist.
23 Presumably the artist's father.
24 The artist's sister Anne (1572–1624) married Sir Robert Drury of Hawstead.
25 It is notable to find here the portrait of a gardener, though it has not yet proved possible to identify the sitter.
26 One of the earliest documentary references to specific paintings by the artist.